I1028898

Heroes and Villains

Anne Frank

Anne Frank

Other books in the Heroes and Villains series include:

Al Capone
Frederick Douglass
Adolf Hitler
Saddam Hussein
Martin Luther King Jr.
King Arthur
Nelson Mandela
Josef Mengele
Oskar Schindler

Heroes and Villains

Anne Frank

Adam Woog

LUCENT
BOOKS ®

THOMSON

GALE

San Diego • Detroit • New York • San Francisco • Cleveland • New Haven. Conn. • Waterville. Maine • London • Munich

© 2004 by Lucent Books. Lucent Books is an imprint of The Gale Group, Inc.,
a division of Thomson Learning, Inc.

Lucent Books® and Thomson Learning™ are trademarks used herein under license.

For more information, contact
Lucent Books
27500 Drake Rd.
Farmington Hills, MI 48331-3535
Or you can visit our Internet site at http://www.gale.com

ALL RIGHTS RESERVED.
No part of this work covered by the copyright hereon may be reproduced or used in any form or
by any means—graphic, electronic, or mechanical, including photocopying, recording, taping,
Web distribution or information storage retrieval systems—without the written permission of
the publisher.

LIBRARY OF CONGRESS CATALOGING-IN-PUBLICATION DATA

Woog, Adam, 1953–
   Anne Frank / by Adam Woog.
      p. cm. — (Heroes and Villains series)
Includes index.
Summary: A biography of Anne Frank, including the historical events that forced
her to hide with her family in an attic in Nazi-occupied Holland for two years.
   ISBN 1-59018-349-5 (alk. paper)
   1. Frank, Anne, 1929–1945—Juvenile literature. 2. Jewish children in the
Holocaust—Netherlands—Amsterdam—Biography—Juvenile literature. 3. Jews—
Netherlands—Amsterdam—Biography—Juvenile literature. 4. Amsterdam
(Netherlands)—Biography—Juvenile literature. [1. Frank, Anne, 1929–1945.
2. Jews—Netherlands—Biography. 3. Holocaust, Jewish (1929–1945)—Netherlands—
Amsterdam. 4. Women—Biography.] I. Title. II. Series.
   DS135.N6F73875 2004
   940.53'18'092—dc22

                             2003018767

Printed in the United States of America

Contents

Foreword

Good and evil are an ever-present feature of human history. Their presence is reflected through the ages in tales of great heroism and extraordinary villainy. Such tales provide insight into human nature, whether they involve two people or two thousand, for the essence of heroism and villainy is found in deeds rather than in numbers. It is the deeds that pique our interest and lead us to wonder what prompts a man or woman to perform such acts.

Samuel Johnson, the eminent eighteenth-century English writer, once wrote, "The two great movers of the human mind are the desire for good, and fear of evil." The pairing of desire and fear, possibly two of the strongest human emotions, helps explain the intense fascination people have with all things good and evil—and by extension, heroic and villainous.

People are attracted to the person who reaches into a raging river to pull a child from what could have been a watery grave for both, and to the person who risks his or her own life to shepherd hundreds of desperate black slaves to safety on the Underground Railroad. We wonder what qualities these heroes possess that enable them to act against self-interest, and even their own survival. We also wonder if, under similar circumstances, we would behave as they do.

Evil, on the other hand, horrifies as well as intrigues us. Few people can look upon the drifter who mutilates and kills a neighbor or the dictator who presides over the torture and murder of thousands of his own citizens without feeling a sense of revulsion. And yet, as Joseph Conrad writes, we experience "the fascination of the abomination." How else to explain the overwhelming success of a book such as Truman Capote's *In Cold Blood*, which examines in horrifying detail a vicious and senseless murder that took place in the American heartland in the 1960s? The popularity of murder mysteries and Court TV are also evidence of the human fascination with villainy.

Most people recoil in the face of such evil. Yet most feel a deep-seated curiosity about the kind of person who could commit a terrible act. It is perhaps a reflection of our innermost fears that we wonder whether we could resist or stand up to such behavior in our presence or even if we ourselves possess the capacity to commit such terrible crimes.

The Lucent Books Heroes and Villains series capitalizes on our fascination with the perpetrators of both good and evil by introducing readers to some of history's most revered heroes and hated villains. These include heroes such as Frederick Douglass, who knew firsthand the humiliation of slavery and, at great risk to himself, publicly fought to abolish the institution of slavery in America. It also includes villains such as Adolf Hitler, who is remembered both for the devastation of Europe and for the murder of 6 million Jews and thousands of Gypsies, Slavs, and others whom Hitler deemed unworthy of life.

Each book in the Heroes and Villains series examines the life story of a hero or villain from history. Generous use of primary and secondary source quotations gives readers eyewitness views of the life and times of each individual as well as enlivens the narrative. Notes and annotated bibliographies provide stepping-stones to further research.

THE SPIRIT OF ANNE FRANK

In the years since World War II, Anne Frank has become a lasting symbol of the courage and hope shown by the millions who endured that war's hardships. Despite terrible burdens and the daily threats of brutality and terror, Anne's heroic optimism about the future, and about humanity in general, continues to shine through. In one of the final entries in her famous diary, she wrote, "It's a wonder I haven't abandoned all my ideals, they seem so absurd and impractical. Yet I cling to them because I still believe, in spite of everything, that people are truly good at heart."[1]

The Nazis

Anne Frank was the most famous victim of the terror known as the Holocaust. This was the program of systematic mass executions conducted by the Nazi Party, which controlled Germany in the years before and during World War II.

The Nazis blamed the Jews and other minorities for everything that was wrong with Germany, and with Europe in general. They devised a "Final Solution," a plan to rid Europe of anyone opposed to them, or deemed "inferior" to their blond, blue-eyed physical ideal. Hitler repeatedly referred to the Jews in such terms as "weak and bestial," "as stupid as they are forgetful," or "lazy and cowardly."[2]

As the war raged on and Germany sought to control Europe, some 6 million Jews were killed, along with other groups deemed unsuitable—the mentally and physically disabled, homosexuals, Gypsies, Slavs (especially Poles and Soviet prisoners of war), Communists, and others. Some were murdered immediately; many more were held in brutal concentration camps, where they died of starvation or disease, or were killed and burned in giant crematoriums.

Hiding

Although millions of Jews died in the Holocaust, millions more survived. They fled before it was too late, or they hid out, or they somehow lived through the horrors of the camps long enough to be freed.

Anne Frank was not one of the survivors. A few months before her sixteenth birthday, she died of typhus in the concentration camp at Bergen-Belsen. She avoided capture by the Nazis for a long time, however. As a thirteen-year-old, in the summer of 1942, Anne went into hiding in a tiny secret annex above her father's

Pictured is an early entry and photograph from the now-famous diary Anne Frank kept during the two years she and her family spent in hiding from the Nazis.

Dit is een foto, zoals ik me zou wensen, altijd zo te zijn. Dan had ik nog wel een kans om naar Holywood te komen.

Anne Frank.
10 Oct. 1942

(translation)
"This is a photo as I would wish myself to look all the time. Then I would maybe have a chance to come to Hollywood."
         Anne Frank, 10 Oct. 1942

"The Most Famous Holocaust Survivor"

In this passage, Rabbi Julia Neuberger reflects on the meaning of Anne Frank as a true survivor. The excerpt is from Anne Frank in the World, *a book created by the curators of Anne Frank House in Amsterdam:*

A few years ago, I was talking to a school group about being Jewish and what that meant to me. After I had explained that my mother was a refugee from Nazi Germany, a child asked me whether I thought Anne Frank was the most famous Holocaust survivor. I was stunned by the question. After all, Anne Frank perished in Bergen-Belsen in 1945, age fifteen. But the more I thought about it, the more I realized that the boy was right. Anne Frank is the most famous Holocaust survivor. But what survived was her diary, an intimate journal that led to her memory becoming in some way eternal, as people came to understand what the war against the Jews meant through the words of one young teenager.

business in the Dutch city of Amsterdam. Seven others joined her, including her parents and her sister Margot.

These eight people spent more than two years tucked away in the annex, living in constant fear and deprivation, but in relative safety, until someone betrayed them in the summer of 1944. The Nazis sent all eight to concentration camps. Anne's father Otto Frank was the only one to return.

The story of Anne Frank is, in many ways, not unique. Millions of others suffered similar fates during the terrible war years. Families lost loved ones; entire families were wiped out; and even those who survived the deprivations of the war were left with horrifying, permanent memories. However, the Frank family's story

has become familiar worldwide for one simple reason: Anne kept a diary.

The Diary

On one level, Anne's diary records the emotions of a normal, middle-class adolescent: somewhat self-centered, quick to criticize, often concerned with trivial matters, and preoccupied with the changes brought by puberty. Writer Ernst Schnabel notes of this normality, "Anne was a child, and not one of [those who knew her] claimed that she had been a prodigy, in any way out of the ordinary."[3] However, because of the turbulent times Anne lived in, and because of her strange circumstances, her diary takes on extraordinary dimensions for modern readers. For one thing, it recorded life in the secret annex, a life that was by turns bizarre, terrifying, and cozily familiar. The diary gives modern readers a glimpse of ordinary people living through extraordinary times. Writer Anna Quindlen notes:

The struggle for identity, the fears, the doubts, above all the everyday-

ness in the diary entries, the worries about outgrown shoes, the romantic yearnings, and the ever-present conflicts with Mama and Margot reflect, mirror, and elevate the lives of millions who went about the business of studying, romancing, cooking, sewing and struggling to live in

A British soldier reads a commemorative billboard outside the Nazi concentration camp at Bergen-Belsen where Anne Frank died of typhus just before her sixteenth birthday.

the world until the Nazis ended their millions of ordinary, individual lives.[4]

Anne's diary entries also clearly document her emotional growth from a bright, young girl into a maturing woman struggling to find her identity. In the two years covered by her journal, Anne grew into a young adult with complex emotions, a thoughtful mind, and a surprisingly mature writing style. This evolution might be true for any person her age keeping a journal, but Anne's circumstances give the story great poignancy.

Finally, her writing about the horrors of war, and about human nature in general, illustrates her passionate belief that, despite everything, the world is essentially a good place. Writers Ann Birstein and Alfred Kazin comment, "What she saw when she looked [through the window of the annex] was a reminder that despite all the ugliness inflicted on it, the world was still incredibly beautiful, and each time she could not get over the miracle of it."[5]

A Diary for the World

In time, Anne began writing for others; she wanted to be published, and her goal was to become a professional writer. At first, however, her diary was strictly for herself; Anne could not believe that anyone else would want to read it. As she noted in one entry, "Sometimes I think God is trying to test me, now and in the future. Who else but me is ever going to read these letters?"[6]

Of course, just the opposite has come true. Her diary has been read by tens of millions and in dozens of languages. It has inspired plays, music, and countless other memorials. It continues to be one

Thinking of Beauty

Anne's diary has many passages about ordinary life, but also many that are musings about more abstract ideas. This diary excerpt is reprinted in Henry F. Pommer's essay "The Legend and Art of Anne Frank," in A Tribute to Anne Frank.

The best remedy for those who are afraid, lonely, or unhappy is to go outside, somewhere where they can be quite alone with the heavens, nature, and God. Because only then does one feel that all is as it should be and that God wishes to see people happy, amidst the simple beauty of nature. As long as this exists, and it certainly always will, I know that there will always be comfort for every sorrow, whatever the circumstances may be. And I firmly believe that nature brings solace in all troubles.

"Oh, Why Are People So Crazy?"

Many of Anne's diary entries are reflections on the war—its causes, its possible outcomes, and its absurdities. In May 1944, for example, as quoted in The Diary of a Young Girl: The Definitive Edition, *Anne Frank wrote:*

As you can no doubt imagine, we often say in despair, "What's the point of the war? Why, oh, why can't people live together peacefully? Why all this destruction?"

The question is understandable, but up to now no one has come up with a satisfactory answer. Why is England manufacturing bigger and better airplanes and bombs and at the same time churning out new houses for reconstruction? Why are millions spent on the war each day, while not a penny is available for medical science, artists or the poor? Why do people have to starve when mountains of food are rotting away in other parts of the world? Oh, why are people so crazy?

of the most popular books ever written about World War II. As a result, Anne's extraordinary spirit continues to survive long after her death and, for that matter, long after the collapse of the Nazi regime. Anne Frank's small voice speaks of the courage and life force inherent in all people, especially those who experienced the Holocaust, and those who today face prejudice and hate.

Chapter One

LIFE BEFORE CONFINEMENT

Anneliese Marie Frank was born into a comfortable, middle-class Jewish household on June 12, 1929, in Frankfurt, Germany. Frankfurt, one of Germany's largest cities, was a lively center of commercial, intellectual, and artistic life. Next to Berlin, it had the largest Jewish community in Germany.

Anne's father Otto Frank had studied at the University of Heidelberg. After that, he worked briefly in New York City and then, back in Germany, for an engineering company. After serving as an officer in the German army during World War I, Otto began working at the bank his family had founded.

In 1925, Otto married Edith Holländer. Like Otto, Edith was the child of an affluent German Jewish family. Competent, quiet, and unassuming, she was a rather traditional German woman for her time.

Their first daughter Margot was born in 1926, followed by Anne three years later.

A Close Family

The Frank family was very closely knit. Otto and Edith Frank were extremely devoted to their children. This was somewhat unusual, considering the times and the family's social position; parents like the Franks were typically uninvolved in their children's daily lives, leaving the task of child rearing to nannies and nursemaids. Contrary to this norm, family friends recall, the Frank home was always full of the girls' toys and drawings, which were never tucked out of sight. Furthermore, the children were always at the center of any activity.

Unlike many fathers of his generation, Otto Frank was especially involved in his children's lives. He took them for walks and excursions. He was an avid photographer, and Anne and Margot were frequently his subjects. He loved to tell them jokes and he began a tradition of writing each girl a poem on her birthday.

Otto also told his daughters stories every night. These often centered on two girls, both named Paula. One was good and the other, mischievous and disobedient. The two Paulas reflected, at least in part, the Frank girls in real life. Margot was quiet, studious, and obedient. Anne, in contrast, was a strong-willed, energetic, and charming child who talked nonstop, challenged her parents on many occasions, and was always into mischief. Her charm and liveliness, combined with a quick smile and an infectious laugh, usually helped her get what she wanted.

A Comfortable Life

When Anne was an infant, the Franks were financially comfortable. They lived in a succession of large, sunny apartments with gardens, in a neighborhood of Frankfurt called Marbachweg. Marbachweg had a pleasant, small-town atmosphere, and the Franks were close to parks and hills with excellent walking paths and trails.

As many cities did, and still do, Frankfurt had neighborhoods that were predominantly one ethnic group or another. Its large Jewish community was already well established. However, the Franks preferred the mixed setting of Marbachweg. Margot and Anne thus grew up around Jews and Gentiles. Otto recognized the importance of understanding the richness of Jewish culture.

The infant Anne Frank (center) poses for a portrait with her father Otto and her sister Margot.

17

A Warm, Inviting Home

The Frank family's home in Amsterdam was a comfortable apartment that they would soon leave behind forever. In this excerpt from Anne Frank Remembered, *friend, employee, and future helper Miep Gies describes her first visit:*

The apartment's furnishings had been brought from Frankfurt, and there were many antiques, mostly in polished, dark woods. . . . A stately old grandfather clock ticked softly in the background. The clock was an Ackerman, made in Frankfurt. When we admired the clock, [Mr.] Frank told us that when it was wound every three to four weeks, it kept precise time.

My eye caught a dreamy charcoal sketch hanging in a fine frame on the wall. It was of a large cat with two little kittens beside her. The mother cat was serene, and the two babies were snuggled against her fur, nursing. The Franks were cat lovers. And indeed, a friendly cat marched possessively across the room as though she owned the place. [Mr.] Frank commented that the cat belonged to his daughters. Everywhere were signs that children dominated this house: drawings, playthings.

However, he also insisted that his daughters be raised in an atmosphere of diversity and acceptance of others.

This attitude went along with the family's generally relaxed religious views. Although Edith had been raised in a traditional Jewish household, Otto had not. He had not had a bar mitzvah, the traditional ritual marking adulthood, and he rarely attended synagogue or observed holidays. He once observed that this was true for the rest of his family: "My grandmother never went to synagogue, except once, to be married."[7]

Hard Times

The Franks' comfortable life did not last long, for several reasons. Germany's overall economy was in ruins. The Great Depression, which began in America in 1929, had hit other parts of the world years earlier. Times were especially bad in Germany.

Throughout the 1920s, Germany suffered great hardships. A major reason for this stemmed from the end of World War I a decade earlier. Held responsible for that war, Germany was forced to pay other nations billions of dollars in reparations. This crushing debt had led to economic ruin. All across Germany, workers lost their jobs, farmers lost their land, and businesses closed. Ordinary people saw their savings disappear as bank after bank failed. Unemployment rose as high as 25 percent.

The country was also experiencing runaway inflation. (Inflation occurs when prices rise faster than wages and people can therefore no longer afford to buy things.) In 1919 one U.S. dollar was worth about nine German marks; by 1923 one dollar was equal to 4 trillion marks. German money was so worthless that coins were most valuable as scrap metal; paper money was used as wallpaper or as fuel in stoves.

Like all Germans, the Frank family suffered from the effects of this ruined economy. Although their family-owned

Elected chancellor of Germany in 1933, the head of the Nazi Party Adolf Hitler sought to systematically exterminate the Jews and other supposedly inferior races.

bank did not fail, neither could it prosper. When Anne was still an infant, the Franks were forced to economize. They moved into a series of progressively smaller apartments and in time had to share Otto's mother's house instead of maintaining their own place.

The Nazis

As Germany's economy failed, and poverty and unemployment spread, the German people became increasingly disillusioned. Many of them searched for someone to blame for their troubles, and many found a scapegoat in the Jewish people. Throughout Germany, there was a rising tide of anti-Semitism (anti-Jewish feeling) that resulted in mounting prejudice and violence against Jews.

One group, in particular, actively fostered anti-Semitism. This was an increasingly powerful political party, the National Socialist German Workers' Party. The Nazis, as the group was called, had exist-

ed since the chaotic aftermath of World War I.

The Nazis preached the fanatical message that Germany's tough economic times were due to foreign-born agitators. The Nazis believed that enemies from within were destroying their country by undermining the economy and sowing the seeds of anarchy. Everyone was suspect, except those whom the Nazis believed to have superior (that is, pure Germanic) breeding. The worst of all the alleged agitators, they believed, were the Jews.

Leading the Nazi Party was Adolf Hitler, an Austrian-born high school dropout, a failed carpenter and fine art painter, and an ex-army corporal. Hitler discovered he had a gift for oratory. His charisma was so strong, moreover, that he was able to motivate large groups of people with speeches denouncing Jews and other so-called foreign elements.

Hitler was thus able to gain the support of many Germans, especially from

"Our State Without Jews"

As the Nazi Party grew in power in Germany, its anti-Semitic message became clearer and bolder, and the rights of Jews were steadily restricted. This passage, from Martin Gilbert's book Never Again, *quotes the official newspaper of the Nazi Party, which in 1933 declared:*

All the suggestions for a lasting status, a lasting regulation of the Jews in Germany, fail to solve the Jewish question, in as much as they fail to rid Germany of the Jews. . . . We must build up our State without Jews. They can never be anything but stateless aliens, they can never have any legal or constitutional powers.

the working class. They helped transform the Nazis from a fringe political movement into a genuine force in the German government. Although many Germans deplored the rise of this right-wing, fanatical element, the Nazis steadily gained power.

Hitler was prepared to be completely ruthless to achieve his goals of controlling Germany and freeing it from those he considered undesirable elements. This ruthlessness was demonstrated by a massacre known as the Night of the Long Knives, in June 1933, when hundreds of members of Hitler's own paramilitary unit, the *Sturmabteilung* or SA, were murdered on his orders. This group, known as the Brownshirts because of its uniforms, had been threatening to seize too much power of its own.

Throughout the 1920s, as the economic situation worsened, the Nazis gained victory after victory in local and national elections. In 1933, Hitler was elected chancellor, making him the country's second-most powerful leader. He swiftly assumed more power, and within eighteen months the führer ("leader"), as he was called, had complete control of Germany.

Hitler outlawed all other political parties and sent those who opposed him to prison. He also banned any news or art that did not reflect Nazi ideals. And he relentlessly promoted an unreasonable hatred of Jews, an emotion echoed in these words from his autobiography, *Mein Kampf:*

Was there any shady undertaking, any form of foulness, especially in cultural life, in which at least one Jew did not participate? On putting the probing knife carefully to that kind of abscess, one immediately discovered, like a maggot in a putrescent [decaying] body, a little Jew who was often blinded by the sudden light.[8]

Anti-Semitism Everywhere

Under Hitler's rule, anti-Semitism became official government policy. A seemingly endless list of laws, added to almost daily, systematically isolated and punished German Jews throughout the 1930s. Some of these laws were simply bizarre. In one case, Jews were forbidden to own pigeons. Other laws seemed designed primarily to humiliate. For example, Jews were required to wear yellow six-pointed star patches on their clothes. (The six-pointed star, called the Star of David, is an important Jewish symbol.) The penalty for appearing in public without the star was imprisonment or worse.

Other laws served to isolate Jews from the rest of the population. Many store and restaurant owners refused to serve Jews, hanging signs on their doors that read, "No Jews Allowed." Meanwhile, non-Jews, often called Gentiles, were forbidden to shop in Jewish-owned stores or to consult Jewish doctors or lawyers.

The laws restricting Jews continued to mount. Jewish business owners were forced to sell their businesses to Gentiles

Nazi soldiers sing anti-Semitic songs in front of a Woolworth store in 1933. The state-sponsored persecution Jews faced forced many to leave Germany in the early 1930s.

at ludicrously low prices, and all Jewish employees were fired from those businesses. Also, Jewish teachers were no longer permitted to teach in public schools.

Physical violence against Jews became increasingly common. Shops were looted and businesses destroyed. Individuals were savagely attacked. The *Manchester Guardian* reported from Berlin in the spring of 1933 that many Jews were beaten by Nazi thugs "until the blood streamed down their heads and faces, and their backs and shoulders were bruised. Many fainted and were left lying in the streets."[9]

Fleeing Germany

Some German Jews refused to believe that the persecution would last. Many optimistically compared it to the fever of an illness from which Germany would eventually recover. Surely, many German Jews felt, the madness their country was experiencing under the Nazis would pass quickly.

Others, however, recognized the growing danger. After all, Jews had been persecuted for centuries at various times all across Europe. In the two thousand years from the beginning of the Roman Empire to the creation of modern Europe, no Jewish community had ever had a completely peaceful existence. Time and again, various local rulers, religious leaders, or communities of citizens had risen up against Jews, punished them, and in some cases driven them away.

Many people made plans to leave Germany. One such person was Otto Frank. At first, like many German Jews, Otto had believed that Nazism would soon blow over and the country would return to normal. However, as the Nazis became more and more powerful, he was also realistic enough to foresee that serious danger was on its way. Hitler had

clearly issued his warning that the destruction of the Jews was imminent, and in time Otto took the threat seriously.

Otto considered fleeing to several countries: Switzerland, where his sister lived, or France, England, or America, where he also had relatives. In the end, he chose the Netherlands. This country, on Germany's northwest border, is often referred to as Holland; its residents are known as the Dutch.

There were several reasons why Otto chose the Netherlands. It was nearby, and

Europe in 1935
BEFORE GERMAN EXPANSION UNDER HITLER

its customs were not too different from those with which his family was familiar. Most important, the Netherlands had a reputation for tolerating Jews. In 1933 Otto made arrangements to move to Amsterdam, the Netherlands' largest city and a place he knew well from previous business trips.

A New Home

In later years, Jews would be forbidden to leave Germany, but in 1933 it was still possible to cross the border. Otto went alone by train to Amsterdam, leaving his family at his mother-in-law's house in the town of Aachen, near the Dutch border. He wanted to set up a business in advance. This was to be a new venture: a branch of Opekta, a German company that manufactured pectin, an ingredient used in making jam. Otto also found an apartment, and, by February 1934, the family was together again at 37 Merwedeplein (Merwede Square), on the third floor of a house in a new residential complex.

Amsterdam was a good place for children. Since Amsterdammers rely largely on bicycles and trams, there were relatively few cars, so Anne and Margot could safely play in the streets. Also, there were many new housing projects in their neighborhood, and families with young children, including a number of German Jewish refugees, were moving in. Furthermore, Amsterdam was close to popular holiday resorts along the Netherlands' North Sea coast, and the family could vacation there easily.

Finally, the country seemed like it would be a safe place for Jews. The Netherlands had (and still has) a reputation for tolerance of different religions, beliefs, and lifestyles. In the fifteenth century, it was a haven for Spanish Jews from the tyranny of the Inquisition. Later, the English Pilgrims found respite there before moving on to America. Biographer Melissa Müller writes, "Dutch Jews were not just tolerated but integrated and respected."[10]

Transition to a New Life

Moving to a new country is often stressful. It is frequently necessary to learn new languages, adjust to different customs, make new friends, and abandon old ones. However, a number of factors eased this difficult transition for the Franks.

One such factor was the city's flourishing Jewish community. Of the one hundred thousand Jews in the mid-1930s Netherlands, half lived in Amsterdam. Although religion did not dominate the Franks' lives, they enjoyed belonging to a synagogue, which served as a cultural community center and made them feel at home in their new country. In particular, the Franks' own neighborhood in the southern part of Amsterdam was a hub for expatriate German Jews.

Another factor easing the transition was finances: Otto's business was reasonably successful. In fact, he did well enough that he was able to form another company, Pectacon, to manufacture and sell

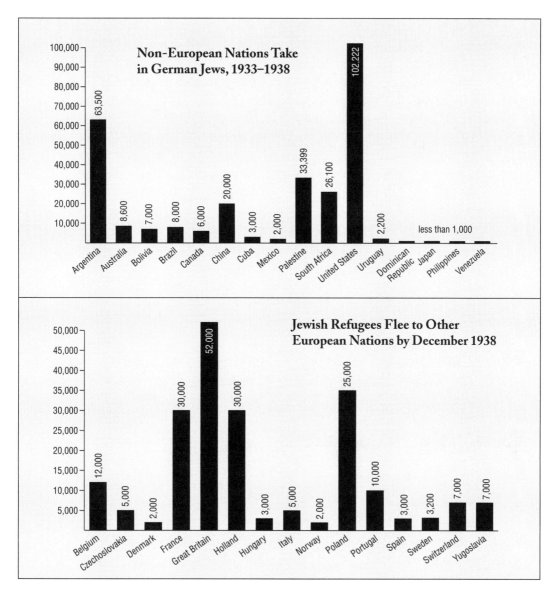

Non-European Nations Take in German Jews, 1933–1938

Nation	Number
Argentina	63,500
Australia	8,600
Bolivia	7,000
Brazil	8,000
Canada	6,000
China	20,000
Cuba	3,000
Mexico	2,000
Palestine	33,399
South Africa	26,100
United States	102,222
Uruguay	2,200
Dominican Republic	less than 1,000
Japan	less than 1,000
Philippines	less than 1,000
Venezuela	less than 1,000

Jewish Refugees Flee to Other European Nations by December 1938

Nation	Number
Belgium	12,000
Czechoslovakia	5,000
Denmark	2,000
France	30,000
Great Britain	52,000
Holland	30,000
Hungary	3,000
Italy	5,000
Norway	2,000
Poland	25,000
Portugal	10,000
Spain	3,000
Sweden	3,200
Switzerland	7,000
Yugoslavia	7,000

spices used in making sausages. The two businesses shared office and warehouse space in an old building at 263 Prinsengracht. To help with his second business, Otto took on a partner, another Jewish refugee from Germany named Hermann van Pels.

Adjusting to Amsterdam

Still another reason for the easy transition to their new home was the quick adaptation the Frank girls made to their new surroundings. They soon learned Dutch, and they easily made friends, both Jewish and Gentile, in their neighborhood and at the private school they attended.

Always lively and bright, Anne loved social activities; she especially liked skating, reading, and going to Oasis, the local ice cream parlor, with her friends. Anne was generally a popular child with adults as well as with other children. Her first-grade teacher recalled, "In many things she was very mature, but on the other hand, in other things she was unusually childish. The combination of these two characteristics made her very attractive."[11]

Anne did reasonably well in school, although her grades were not especially good, and she was often in trouble for talking in class. In fact, she talked so much that her teachers and classmates nick-named her "Chatterbox." In contrast, studious and quiet Margot always did much better academically than her sister.

Unfortunately, Anne's mother did not adapt as well to their new home. The Franks could no longer afford to hire a maid, nanny, or cook, so Edith had all of the housework and child care on her shoulders. She tried to learn Dutch, but, discouraged with its difficulty, gave up her studies. Also, because Otto was often away on business, she was lonely.

Overall, Edith Frank was depressed and homesick for the life she had known in Frankfurt. Miep Gies, Otto Frank's employee and soon to be their helper in hiding, recalls:

Mrs. Frank missed Germany a great deal, much more than Mr. Frank. In conversation she would very often refer with melancholy to their life in Frankfurt, to the superiority of some kinds of German sweets and the

Skating

Anne adjusted easily to her new life in the Netherlands. For example, in a letter from early 1941, as quoted in Melissa Müller's Anne Frank: The Biography, *she gave her relatives in Switzerland a detailed report on her experiences with the popular national pastime of ice-skating:*

I spend every free minute I have at the rink. Until now I'd been using Margot's old skates that I had to attach to my shoes with a key. All my friends at the rink had real figure-skates with the blades attached to the shoes with little nails so they can't come off. . . .

After pestering my parents for a long time I got new skates, and now I'm taking lessons in figure skating. We're learning to waltz on skates, to jump, and all kinds of other things. I gave my old skates to Hanneli [Goslar, a friend] and she is very pleased with them, so now both of us are happy.

quality of German clothing. . . .
[She] liked to reminisce about the
past, about her happy childhood in
the small city of Aachen, her mar-
riage to Mr. Frank in 1925, and their
life in Frankfurt.[12]

War Begins

By the late 1930s, the Nazis were becoming extremely aggressive toward other
countries. It appeared certain that Germany
would soon try to grow beyond its borders.
This fit in with Hitler's ambitious plans to
expand his empire, creating vast areas of
Lebensraum (living space) that would be
exclusively for the German people.

His first move was to occupy Austria
and Czechoslovakia, which he did without bloodshed. Then, in the summer of
1939, he invaded Poland. The Poles were
so unprepared for the invasion that, in
some cases, armed with nothing but horses and spears, they were forced to go
against German tanks. The massive
German army quickly overwhelmed this
valiant but doomed group.

In the wake of this brutal invasion,
Great Britain and France, who had
formed an alliance with Poland, declared
war against Germany. World War II officially began; the threat of open conflict,
which had been hanging over Europe for
years, was now reality. Denmark and
Norway were the next to fall to the Nazis.
Then, in May 1940, Germany invaded
Belgium, Luxembourg, France, and the
Netherlands.

Restricting the Jews

The attack on their country took the
Dutch by complete surprise. They had
expected to remain neutral in the war, as
they had in World War I, and were simply not equipped to mount a serious
counterattack against the Germans. A
few anti-Nazi strikes and protests were
organized, but were quickly and brutally
suppressed. Government officials and the
Dutch royal family were forced to flee to
England. Within weeks, the Germans
had complete control of the country.

One of the first measures the Germans took was to impose regulations
against Jews. In the years before the war,
the number of Jews in the Netherlands
had increased dramatically from the pre-
war figure of 100,000. By 1940 the population of Dutch Jews had grown to about
140,000, of whom roughly 24,000 were
German refugees.

The anti-Semitic laws already in place in
Germany were adapted for the Netherlands.
Dutch Jews were forbidden, for instance, to
enter all public places, including parks,
swimming pools, movie theaters, markets,
and shops. They had to wear yellow stars,
and businesses were forcibly taken over.
They were also gradually moved from their
homes into ghettos (restricted neighborhoods), separated from their neighbors by
barbed wire fences. Dutch Jews were even
banned from owning or riding bicycles. This
was a serious issue in the Netherlands,
where so many people depended on bicycles for transportation. All Jews were
ordered to hand over to the authorities their

The Third Reich, 1938

Annexed by Germany, 1938

Europe by January 1, 1939

bicycles, in perfect condition and equipped with spare tires.

The Family Affected

Such restrictions deeply affected the Frank family. In some cases the Franks rebelled slightly, as did many others. For instance, they put their bicycles in storage instead of turning them in to the authorities. In other ways, however, the Franks bowed to pressure in an effort to avoid problems for the family. For example, they removed Anne and Margot from their school, where the girls had been very happy, and, as they were ordered, sent them instead to a special school for Jews.

Anne was allowed to run errands for her mother, such as going to the store, only between the Nazi-determined hours of 3:00 P.M. and 5:00 P.M., and only in stores marked as "Jewish shops." In keeping with the curfew for Jews, she could not go to the movies, play tennis, go swimming, or go outside after 8:00 P.M. Nor could she ride on a train, eat in a restaurant, or visit openly with her Christian friends.

In 1940 Otto Frank was forced to "Aryanize" his business, that is, to sell it to a non-Jew. (The Aryan race was the allegedly superior bloodline championed by the Nazis.) Otto signed his business over to someone he already worked with and trusted, Victor Kugler. Kugler was Dutch and a Christian, although he was no friend of the Nazis. Otto now officially was unemployed, but, thanks to his friendship with Kugler, he could remain in charge behind the scenes.

"We're Not Likely to Get Sunburned"

Despite the worsening situation, the Franks tried to keep life as normal as possible. For example, it was bothersome for Anne to be barred from theaters, because she passionately loved movies. The Franks tried to solve the problem by renting pro-jectors and films for screenings in their home on special occasions.

Such occasions were excuses for the Franks to lavish extra attention on their daughters, perhaps in an attempt to make up for the deprivations elsewhere in their lives. For instance, on her birthday in 1941, Anne received more presents than ever before and she happily reported in a letter to her grandmother that the dining room table was piled with presents. On the other hand, Anne complained in another letter, dated that summer, about a particularly irritating aspect of her limited activities: "We're not likely to get sunburned, because we can't go to the swimming pool. Too bad, but there's nothing to be done."[13]

Soon enough, she had more to worry about than sunburns. In 1942 the occu-pying government began to deport Dutch Jews, sending them to concentration

The Inferior and Superior Races

In his book The Dutch Under German Occupation 1940–1945, *historian Werner Warmbrunn examines many aspects of his topic. In this excerpt he comments on the origins of the Nazi theories about racial superiority:*

[The Nazis] recognized two main racial groups: first, the Aryan race, represented by what the linguists call the Indo-European peoples, and second, all other races. . . . The Nordic and Germanic peoples were considered the most valuable races and were described as the creators of all important civilizations and the founders of all powerful states. . . .

National Socialist doctrine asserted that the Aryan races had an implacable enemy in the Jewish race, the "anti-Race," which, it charged, tried to destroy the substance and achievements of the higher races, through deceit and . . . exploitation of the host nation.

camps where they would be forced into slave labor or brutally exterminated. This was to be done as efficiently as possible, as the head of the Dutch branch of the Gestapo (the Nazi political police force) told his organization: "It is my endeavor to dispose of the Jews as quickly as possible. This is not a pretty assignment, but it is a great work. . . . Whoever does not understand this and speaks of pity and humanism cannot be a leader in these times."[14]

Unemployed male Jews were the first to go, but the orders soon included a wider circle slated to include all Jews. This deportation measure was what finally forced the Frank family to take the drastic step of going into hiding.

Chapter Two

The Hiding Begins

No one knew exactly what happened to those who left for the concentration camps spread out over occupied Europe. The Nazis claimed that they were nothing more sinister than labor camps designed to make use of a human workforce. All that the Franks or other Jews in the Netherlands knew, however, was that no one ever returned from them.

People tried a variety of schemes to keep from being deported. A handful of lucky families managed to get visas from other countries that gave them the right to leave German-occupied lands. Others tried to prove that they were not Jewish by claiming that, generations before, their families had become baptized Christians.

Many Jews tried escaping. They left by any means possible: by car, by ship, even by bicycle or on foot. However, escape was difficult and dangerous. The Nazis had sealed the borders of the Netherlands and other occupied countries. Without the proper papers, virtually impossible to obtain, escape attempts frequently ended in imprisonment or death.

For the majority of Dutch Jews, therefore, there was no real chance of escape. For them, every day was an agony of humiliating and hateful restrictions, during which the slightest mistake could lead to a beating or worse. Every night was a long stretch of fearful waiting, hoping that the knock on the door signaling a police roundup would never come.

Diving

Certain that they were coming closer every day to being deported, Otto and Edith Frank seriously considered abandoning the Netherlands. They considered joining Otto's mother, who was by then living in neutral Switzerland; it might have been possible to find a way there. Also, Otto's cousin in England had already offered to take in the girls. However, the Franks chose not to send their daughters abroad alone. Otto wrote to his cousin, "We couldn't bear to part with the girls. They mean too much to us. But if it's any comfort to you, you are the people we would have trusted [with their care]."[15]

To keep his family together, Otto decided the family should stay and go into hiding. He was not the only Jew to consider becoming an *onderduiker*, "one who dives under," as the Dutch had begun calling a Jew in hiding. It has been

A Jewish family in Amsterdam takes their belongings to the train station from which they will be transported to a concentration camp.

estimated that between twenty thousand and thirty thousand Dutch Jews went into hiding between 1942 and 1943. The majority of these "divers" did not stay in the nation's cities, however. Most fled to remote farms in the countryside, where Dutch Gentiles helped them. Farmers hid people in their barns. Some families even took Jewish children into their homes and passed them off as family members.

Hiding was tricky and perilous, and sometimes people seeking help were cheated or betrayed. Sometimes unscrupulous Gentiles charged outrageous sums to hide Jews. There were also instances of Gentiles taking Jews in, then informing on them for a reward.

These were isolated cases, however. For the most part, Gentiles who hid Jews in the Netherlands and elsewhere were generous and brave. These helpers had to share their precious food supplies with the escapees; food was by this time rationed and in extremely short supply. Furthermore, the helpers put their own lives at risk. A Gentile discovered sheltering Jews was usually arrested and sent to a special camp for "traitors."

The Secret Annex

For the Frank family, Otto formulated a bold plan. Rather than find refuge in the countryside, he decided to hide his family right under the noses of the Nazis. Otto realized that sometimes a hiding place can be successful if it is so obvious that no one would ever look there.

The building that housed Otto's business offices and warehouse at 263 Prinsengracht was convenient for this plan. Very close to the old, central part of Amsterdam, it adjoined a blue-collar neighborhood called the Jordaan. The building, dating from the seventeenth century, was nondescript—tall and narrow and made of brick, in the city's typical style. The main building faced a canal, with a second building behind it. An internal passageway connected the two.

Hidden from the general public behind a steep staircase was a tiny annex: four small rooms on two levels, plus an attic. Here Otto created his hideaway. The annex space, Otto calculated, would be big enough for two families. He therefore invited another Jewish family to join his: his business partner, Hermann van Pels,

"They Took Away My Wife"

Anne's childhood friend Hanneli Goslar, quoted in Willy Lindwer's The Last Seven Months of Anne Frank, *recalls some of what it was like for children under the tightening noose of Nazi occupation:*

Jews had to wear a yellow star. We had an *Ausweis* (an identification card), with a large "J" on it—for Jew. People were stopped on the street: "May I see your *Ausweis?*" If you were Jewish, you were taken away and you never returned home. And a mother waiting for her child would ask herself: Where is my child? Have they taken her away?

It became more dangerous every day. And day by day our classroom became emptier. We arrived in the morning and this boy would no longer be there and that girl wouldn't be there. I shall never forget how Mr. Presser, our history teacher . . . gave us a lecture about the Renaissance. He began to read to us about the meeting of [the poet] Dante and [his great love] Beatrice in paradise. Suddenly, in the middle of the lesson, he began to cry and ran out of the class.

"What's the matter?"

"Last night they took away my wife."

van Pels's wife Auguste, and their fifteen-year-old son Peter.

Confederates

Otto knew his plan would be impossible without confederates, people in the "outside" world to supply food and other necessities. He therefore took into his confidence five of his employees: Victor Kugler, on paper, the business's owner; Kugler's assistant Johannes Kleiman; two secretaries, Hermine "Miep" Santrouschitz, better known as Miep Gies, her married name, and Elisabeth "Bep" Voskuijl; and Bep's father, Johannes Voskuijl, the warehouse foreman.

Otto trusted these people to keep his secret. He knew that they were Christians who sympathized with the plight of the Jews. He felt confident that they would prevent the handful of others employed in the warehouse from discovering the

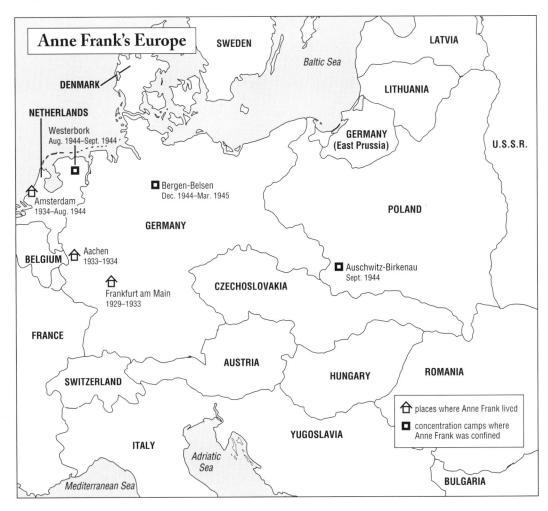

Anne Frank's Europe

SWEDEN

Baltic Sea

LATVIA

DENMARK

LITHUANIA

NETHERLANDS

Westerbork
Aug. 1944–Sept. 1944

GERMANY
(East Prussia)

U.S.S.R.

Bergen-Belsen
Dec. 1944–Mar. 1945

Amsterdam
1934–Aug. 1944

POLAND

GERMANY

Aachen
1933–1934

BELGIUM

Auschwitz-Birkenau
Sept. 1944

Frankfurt am Main
1929–1933

CZECHOSLOVAKIA

FRANCE

AUSTRIA

HUNGARY

ROMANIA

SWITZERLAND

places where Anne Frank lived

concentration camps where Anne Frank was confined

ITALY

Adriatic Sea

YUGOSLAVIA

Mediterranean Sea

BULGARIA

"Their Grief Was Worse"

Thousands of Jewish families were torn apart by the need to hide from the Nazis, in some cases, entrusting their children to strangers. Johannes Bogaard, who risked punishment by the Nazis to hide Jews on his farm, reflects on this in the following passage from Russell Misser's The Resistance:

Can you imagine what that meant to the parents, to give their children to someone they had never seen, whom they knew nothing about, not even his name? I had one family with seven children. Their grief was worse, much worse, than all the danger I ran.

people in hiding. However, Otto did not dare reveal his plans to anyone beyond them. The more people who knew about it, he reasoned, the greater the danger would be. The Germans, after all, were offering rewards to anyone who betrayed hidden Jews. There were such serious food shortages and other hardships in the Netherlands that many people, even those who otherwise would have been sympathetic to Jews, were being driven to betrayal.

Preparing the Annex

The five confederates were more than willing to do what they could to prepare the annex and hide the *onderduikers*. Despite the gravity of the situation and the risks involved, they felt duty-bound to help in any way they could. About Miep Gies, for instance, Melissa Müller writes, "She respected Otto Frank; he was her friend, and not only her friend but also her employer, the most fair-minded employer she could imagine. He was a man to whom anyone would be loyal. It never occurred to her to say no."[16]

Otto, Hermann van Pels, and their confederates outfitted the annex with as many comforts as possible. Over the course of several months, working late at night, the group sneaked household items such as dishes, rugs, bedclothes, clothing, books, and furniture into the hidden rooms. They stockpiled canned and dried food and installed a bathroom with a sink and a toilet.

Johannes Voskuijl, a skilled carpenter, built a pivoting bookcase that concealed the stairway to the annex. This bookcase looked ordinary; it was filled with nondescript gray file folders, and pinned to the wall above it was a simple map of Belgium. But the bookcase could swing outward, revealing a white door above a high step. On the other side was the narrow stairway to the annex.

As an old man, Otto Frank demonstrates how a pivoting bookcase concealed the entrance to the secret annex in which the Frank family hid for more than two years.

A Momentous Present

Otto felt that the annex would be ready by mid-July, and he set July 16, 1942, as the date for moving into it. Before that, however, there was an important anniversary to observe: Anne's thirteenth birthday. As always, the family took special care to plan and celebrate the event.

Anne woke up early that morning; she was so excited that she could hardly contain herself or keep from rousing the others. She later noted, "I was awake at six o'clock, which isn't surprising. . . . But

I'm not allowed to get up at that hour, so I had to control my curiosity until quarter to seven. When I couldn't wait any longer, I went to the dining room, where Moortje (the cat) welcomed me by rubbing against my legs."[17]

According to the family's custom, the dining room table had been loaded down with gifts the night before. On it, among other presents, were books, jewelry, a game, a blouse, a puzzle, money, and candy. Otto probably also gave Anne a poem written in her honor; such poems were a family tradition.

Perhaps the best gift, however—certainly the one that proved to be the most important—was a simple blank book. Its checkered cloth cover closed with a strap and a small lock on the front. A few days before, Anne had pointed it out to her father in a bookstore window. It was designed as an autograph book, but she wanted it to use as a diary.

The book was the perfect gift for someone like Anne, who was bright, imaginative, and able to express herself well on paper. She had already done a lot of writing, mainly little stories and essays, and she was delighted with the chance to do more.

The First Entries

The first entry in Anne's diary was dated Sunday, June 12, 1942, her birthday. She wrote, "I hope I shall be able to confide in you completely, as I have never been able to do in anyone before, and I hope that you will be a great support and comfort to me."[18]

Two days later, Anne made her first long entry in the book, describing the birthday party her family had given her. She listed her presents and described taking to her classmates a batch of cookies she had made. The next entry described a larger party, held for all her friends. This

The Nazis Raid a Neighborhood

Reprinted in Werner Warmbrunn's The Dutch Under German Occupation 1940–1945, *this excerpt from an underground newspaper describes a typical Nazi raid of a Jewish neighborhood in Amsterdam in 1942:*

In the quiet streets of the Zuid [the southern part of Amsterdam] you hear suddenly the noise of many cars, the hated [Nazi] Green Police vans in which the Germans fetch their victims. . . . In a short time [all the streets] have been occupied. . . . And then it begins: on each corner stand German agents, rifles slung across their shoulders. . . . And there they noisily climb upstairs: "Are any Jews living here?" And then the Jews of Holland are driven together on the street corner. . . .

From the fourth floor a Jew leaps to his death rather than fall into the hands of the Germans. The Germans followed him up to the roof after they had searched closets and cellars, attics and tool sheds. A dog who defends his master . . . is shot down by the Germans. . . .

Then comes the end. The big green vans start their engines and begin to move. The engines keep roaring until a quarter to twelve. . . . The vans bring their loads to the Gestapo Building [and the trains] start leaving the city.

Otto Frank's secretary Miep Gies helped the Frank family during their stay in the secret annex.

celebration included the screening of a movie starring one of Anne's favorites, the canine actor Rin Tin Tin. In the same entry, Anne also discussed her friends and classmates, providing a short character sketch of each.

By June 20 Anne had settled on a format for her journal. She would write her entries in the form of letters to an imaginary friend, whom she called "Kitty." (The name came from a character in *Joopter Heul*, a popular novel for young women that Anne had enjoyed.) She noted that she felt as though she did not have a true friend in whom she could confide, but that Kitty could fill that role.

In letters to Kitty, Anne wrote, she would be able to reveal her most personal feelings. She could write whatever she liked. After all, as she noted, it was not very likely that anyone else would ever read them.

The Need to Run

As it turned out, the Franks were forced to enter their hiding place ten days sooner than their planned date of July 16. This was because the dreaded deportation orders finally arrived. Every Dutch newspaper proclaimed that any Jew still in the Netherlands would be relocated to a labor camp. Notices were sent out to one thousand teenagers, the first batch of these deportees.

On July 5, 1942, sixteen-year-old Margot Frank received her notice and was instructed to report to the Nazi authorities immediately. She would be going to Westerbork, known as a transit camp because it was a way station for Dutch Jews headed to other camps. With typical Germanic thoroughness, Margot's orders were very specific; she was to bring two blankets, sheets, enough food to last three days, a towel and toiletries, a plate, a cup, and a spoon. In addition, she was to have a suitcase or backpack with one pair of winter shoes, two pairs of socks, two pairs of underpants, two undershirts, and one pair of overalls. The suitcase had to have her full name, date of birth, and her home country written on it since it would be sent separately. Also, she needed to take all of her ration cards, which entitled her to certain amounts of rationed food, and identification papers.

The Frank family had always expected Otto to be the first deported because he was the adult head of the household. For Margot to receive the first notice was an enormous shock. Edith was the first to read the letter. To protect her daughter, she decided to tell Margot that Otto had been called up. She then left the house to find Hermann van Pels and asked Margot to break the news to Anne gently.

An Emergency Plan

When Edith and Hermann returned to the Franks' home, they discussed the situation throughout the afternoon, but the girls were not allowed to listen. At one point the doorbell rang and everyone jumped. They were all too frightened to answer it, but learned later that it was just Helmuth Silberberg, one of Anne's first boyfriends. He had come to visit Anne, but when no one answered the door he went away.

When Otto arrived home, the three adults finalized their plans. The Franks would disappear immediately, even though the hideout was not completely ready. Hermann van Pels and his family would follow shortly after.

Calmly, Otto and Edith told the girls that they would be leaving their apartment

Always Moving On

British historian Bob Moore, in his book Victims and Survivors: The Nazi Persecution of the Jews in the Netherlands 1940–1945, *points out that the Frank family was unusual in having one place in which to hide indefinitely.*

Although having only one hiding place was not unique, for the vast majority of those underground, remaining in safety usually involved moving around. At the end of the occupation, some survivors could recount 10, 20, or even more places they had hidden for periods of time. A survey of children hidden underground revealed an average number of 4.5 addresses with the highest being 37. . . .

The hiding places varied enormously. Dwelling houses, upstairs rooms in cafés, even buildings used or lived in by the Germans sometimes contained hiding places. False walls and ceilings would conceal cupboards, rooms and even suites of rooms from the casual observer. . . .

In . . . rural areas, hiding places ranged from bunkers dug into the ground in unpopulated areas of heathland [scrub], turf [dirt] shelters and "converted" chickenhouses, through barns and outhouses, to accommodation inside farmhouses.

and going to a hiding place. The adults told their children what they genuinely believed: that they would be away for only several weeks, or perhaps a few months at most. The girls were shocked, but Anne, still in many ways a young child, was more excited that frightened.

That evening, the family packed hastily. Anne and Margot were told to fill their schoolbags as full as possible. They could not take suitcases because they could not risk being seen on the street looking like they were fleeing. Anne tried to pack too much at first— far more than she could carry. She finally chose a mixture of things: her diary,

hair curlers, handkerchiefs, schoolbooks, combs, old letters, clothes, and mementos.

Anne still did not grasp the seriousness of the situation. The idea of departing was an exciting adventure, but also a little frightening, and her emotions that evening veered back and forth from giddiness to fear. Miep Gies, who was helping the family get ready, recalls, "Anne's eyes were like saucers, a mixture of excitement and terrible fright."[19]

Walking into Hiding

Early on the morning of July 6, Edith and Otto woke up their daughters. Anne and Margot were told to put on as many layers of clothing as possible, even though it was not a cold day; since suitcases were out of the question, they needed to wear as much as possible. Anne walked to her new home wearing two undershirts, three pairs of pants, a dress, a skirt, a jacket, a summer coat, two pairs of stockings, sturdy shoes, a woolen cap, and a scarf. As Anne wrote, "We put on heaps of clothes as if we were going to the North Pole, [because] no Jew in our situation would have dreamed of going out with a suitcase full of clothing."[20]

The weather was warm, but there was also a heavy rain that morning. This was a stroke of luck; it meant that fewer people, including the police, would be on

The Franks went into hiding after learning that Margot Frank (pictured) was slated for deportation to a concentration camp.

Remaining Upbeat

Even though things were grim, Otto Frank tried to remain optimistic. In a letter written just before going into hiding, he mentioned that everyone's health was good and made an oblique reference to the family's difficulties. The excerpt is reprinted in Anne Frank: The Biography:

My dear loved ones, All is still well with us, but otherwise things are getting worse from day to day, as you probably know. But don't worry, even if you don't hear much from us. …We are not forgetting about you, and we know that you always think of us, but there is nothing you can do to change things, and you must see to it that you are safe yourselves. With much love as always, your O.

the street. Miep arrived at the apartment at 7:30 A.M., and she and Margot were the first to leave for the Prinsengracht building, traveling by bicycle.

Anne and her parents left on foot a little later. They were carrying satchels and bags filled with various possessions—as many as they thought they could get away with. Walking slowly to avoid suspicion, they took nearly an hour—much longer than usual—to reach 263 Prinsengracht from their apartment in southern Amsterdam.

The Franks deliberately left their apartment in disarray, with beds unmade and food still on the table. An address scribbled on a piece of paper was also left behind as a false clue. The intent was to make it seem that they had fled the country.

Meanwhile, Otto wrote a carefully worded note to his sister Helene in Switzerland, which Miep later mailed: "Dearest Lunni, because we will not be able to write later, we are sending you our birthday wishes now so that they will be sure to reach you in good time. We wish you all the best. We are well and together; that is the main thing."[21] Since Helene ("Lunni") Frank's birthday was not until September, Otto hoped that she would read between the lines and guess the letter's true meaning—that he might not be able to write to her on her birthday because his family was safe but in hiding.

Settling In

Both Edith and Margot collapsed when they reached the annex, too disoriented and frightened by the stress of the situation to be of use. On the other hand, Otto and Anne, helped by Miep, were full of energy and got to work immediately organizing things. There was much to be done, since the move had happened sooner than anyone had expected.

Anne and her father made window coverings out of whatever scraps of cloth

A photo of Anne Frank in hiding shows the young girl at her desk with the diary that would make her the most famous victim of the Holocaust.

they could find, then fastened them in place with thumbtacks. They also fashioned heavy cardboard coverings for the windows to prevent any light from escaping at night. These were blackout curtains. Blackout curtains were used all over the city, so that lights from windows could not guide English and American planes flying overhead. For the Franks, of course, the curtains would serve a second purpose: They would keep passersby from seeing that the annex was occupied after normal working hours.

Anne and her father also moved pieces of furniture into place and scrubbed floors. They rolled out carpets, unpacked boxes and bags, stowed kitchen supplies and books, and did other chores. To her surprise, Anne found pieces of furniture in the annex that had been missing from their old apartment for months; her mother had explained their absence by telling her that they were being repaired.

A Strange New Life

The Franks had left almost everything behind. They had brought with them, literally, little more than the clothes on their backs. Miep Gies writes, "I couldn't begin to imagine what they must be feeling to have walked away from everything they owned in the world—their home; a lifetime of gathered possessions; Anne's little cat, Moortje. Keepsakes from the past. And friends."[22]

However, there were compensations. Anne was pleased, for instance, to find that Otto had brought her collection of postcards and pictures of notable people cut from magazines. Among these were portraits of famous painters, movie stars, and members of various royal families. Otto had sensed that these familiar images might help Anne through the difficult time to come.

On July 8 Anne made the first entry in her diary since entering this new life: "Dearest Kitty, It seems like years since Sunday morning [when she had last written]. So much has happened it's as if the whole world had suddenly turned upside down. But as you can see, Kitty, I'm alive all right, but don't ask where or how."[23]

Anne's life had suddenly and dramatically shrunk. When Miep left the Frank family in the annex on that first day and closed the door behind her, the outside world very nearly disappeared for them. Their new world consisted of nothing but a few hundred square feet of cramped living space. Their new life, meanwhile, would be full of emotions: primarily fear, boredom, and anger, but with occasional flashes of happiness.

Chapter Three

LIFE IN
THE ANNEX

About a week after the Franks arrived, the van Pelses joined them in hiding. The annex now held seven people in four rooms. Otto and Edith had the largest, just above the office. Anne and Margot took the small room next door. Anne brightened its bare walls by covering them with her pictures of royalty and movie stars. Above this floor was Mr. and Mrs. van Pels's room. During the day, this doubled as a kitchen and living room. Peter had the tiny room next door.

The early days of confinement were almost cheerful. Everyone ate together, and Anne liked having another young person around, although Peter, like Margot, was very quiet. Peter's cat Mouschi, which came despite an earlier agreement to bring no animals, was also good company. Anne wrote, "I don't think I'll ever feel at home in this house, but that doesn't mean I hate it. It's more like being on vacation in some strange *pension* [a small hotel]."[24]

An Eighth *Onderduiker*

A few months later, acutely aware that many other Jews were in danger, the Franks and van Pelses decided there was room for one more *onderduiker*. Several candidates were considered before they settled on Albert ("Fritz") Pfeffer, Miep's dentist and a friend of both families.

They asked Miep to invite him, and when Pfeffer arrived everyone was waiting with a coffee-and-cognac celebration. Miep recalls what a surprise it was for the dentist: "Seeing Mr. Frank was [for Pfeffer] like seeing a ghost, because he thought that the Franks had escaped to Switzerland. Who could have imagined that they were right in the center of Amsterdam?"[25]

44

Pfeffer brought the latest news about the outside world. He was able to report, for instance, that the Gestapo searched nightly for Jews, who were taken immediately to the Westerbork transit camp. Miep and the other helpers had until then avoided providing such news, for fear of upsetting their friends too much. Pfeffer also mentioned the rumors circulating in their old neighborhood that the Franks and van Pelses were in Switzerland, or that they had been picked up by the Germans.

The Odd Couple

It was decided that Pfeffer would share Anne's room, taking over Margot's bed. Margot, meanwhile, moved into the elder Franks' room with them. However, Pfeffer and Anne proved to be a bad match as roommates.

Everything about Pfeffer bothered Anne: He snored, he had a know-it-all attitude, and his pompous, humorless manner drove her crazy. (When she disguised identities in her diary, she called him Albert Dussel; *Dussel*, in German, means "idiot" or "fool.") Conversely, Anne's outspokenness and strong nature annoyed Pfeffer. In his opinion, Anne was a child, and children needed to be obedient, quiet, and respectful at all times.

Pairing Anne with a man forty years her senior might seem strange, even considering the extraordinary circumstances. To some historians and biographers, the decision validated Anne's complaint, often voiced in her diary, that the adults

thought of her only as a small child without rights or feelings. Furthermore, Anne was an adolescent, just starting to mature sexually and emotionally; rather than being forced into close proximity with an adult of the opposite sex, she needed as much solitude as possible. Melissa Müller asserts, "Not only Otto but Edith Frank . . . disregarded her growing need for privacy and obviously ignored their adolescent daughter's sense of modesty."[26]

Being Quiet but Busy

Daily life in the annex was relentlessly dangerous, as the slightest mistake could cause everyone's downfall. The hiders could not go near windows. They could not leave trash or any other evidence

Anne's Room

The Dentist in the Toilet

Albert Pfeffer, whom Anne disguises as "Dussel" in her diary, often spent long hours in the toilet, usually as a retreat for reading and studying, especially when the van Pels and Frank families were arguing. In an excerpt from her diary, reprinted in Rabbi Julia Neuberger's introduction to Anne Frank in the World, *she describes teasing him about this:*

Dussel now sits on the "bog," to borrow the expression, every day at twelve thirty on the dot. This afternoon, I boldly took a piece of pink paper and wrote:
Mr. Dussel's Toilet Timetable: Mornings from 7:15 to 7:30 A.M.
Afternoons after 1:00 P.M. Otherwise, only as needed!
I tacked this to the green lavatory door while he was still inside. I might well have added "Transgressors [violators] will be subject to confinement!" because our lavatory door can be locked from both the inside and the outside.

where it might be discovered. Quiet was paramount. Although the helpers knew there were people in the annex, the other employees, such as workers in the warehouse, did not. Also, many people came in and out of the warehouse and offices on business during the course of the day.

For most of the day, therefore, no one in the annex could flush the toilet or run water. If they walked at all, they tiptoed in bedroom slippers. They spoke in whispers, and only when necessary. Even at night, they had to be careful; sounds carried easily in Amsterdam's narrow streets, and they could not risk having noise from a building that was supposedly vacant in the evenings. Anne wrote, "We are as quiet as baby mice. Who, 3 months ago, would have guessed that quicksilver Anne

would have to sit still for hours—and what's more, could?"[27]

It was a strange, sedentary life. When the *onderduikers* started it, they thought the situation would be temporary—a few weeks or months. As the war dragged on, however, so did their confinement. Anne's new life, so different from her former existence, settled into something like routine.

This routine was established largely by Otto, who organized many of the household's practices. Fearing that without regular schedules and tasks any of them might fall into idleness or self-pity, Otto made sure everyone was occupied nearly all the time with something— reading, studying, playing games, or even just scraping carrots for the evening meal.

Mornings

On weekdays, everyone rose by 7 A.M. This gave them about an hour and a half to do chores before the warehouse workers arrived downstairs. During this time, the *onderduikers* removed the blackout cardboard from the windows, washed up, stored bedding, pushed tables and chairs into place, and performed other noisy chores.

Breakfast was at 9:00 A.M. Since they ate in the upstairs common room, they could make a certain amount of noise. Also, by this time they could count on clatter from below, such as typewriting and the grinding of the spice mill, to mask some of the noise they made. The common room and Peter's adjoining bedroom were the only places where they could talk above a whisper, however.

The rest of the morning was spent sewing, reading, knitting, studying, and doing kitchen duty, at which everyone took a turn. Otto was especially concerned that the young people not fall behind academically, so he established a rigorous schedule of study, including languages, math, geography, history, and stenography (a form of shorthand writing). He also made sure that Miep brought them new study materials on a regular basis.

Anne disliked science and math, but her father insisted that she be well-rounded in her studies. (He sometimes threatened to take her diary away if she did not study the hated subjects.) However, she loved history and was a voracious reader of novels and magazines about movie stars. Otto also introduced her to Johann Wolfgang von Goethe, Friedrich Schiller, and other masters of classic German literature.

Margot, always more academic than Anne, enjoyed studies of all kinds. Peter preferred to tinker and repair things in a small workshop he established in the attic, and his parents did not force him to study. However, Otto managed to interest Peter in studying French and English.

The adults frequently studied and read as well. Otto loved Charles Dickens for his humor and social criticism. Also, reading Dickens's work in its original language helped Otto practice his English. Pfeffer studied Spanish; he hoped to immigrate to South America after the war. Edith, meanwhile, liked all kinds of books except detective stories.

Afternoons and Evenings

The high point of the day for Anne was lunchtime, when the workers downstairs had an hour and a half break. During this time, one or more of the helpers, usually Miep, came upstairs. The visitors were always welcome. They brought newspapers, magazines, and fresh food such as produce, meat, milk, and bread. They also brought books, which Jan Gies, Miep's boyfriend (and later husband), brought from the library.

The workers returned to the building at 2:00, and the annex maintained silence again until 5:30. This meant naps and more quiet activities. At the end of the workday,

The eight occupants of the annex were careful to be as quiet as possible. Miep and Jan Gies brought books to help keep them entertained.

everyone could relax a little; they could even venture downstairs, roaming the offices and warehouse with relative freedom. Otto and Hermann could look over the day's business. Anne and Margot could exercise and dance, although Anne had a bad shoulder and had to be cautious she did not injure it. Often, they also did simple office tasks for Miep, such as licking envelopes.

Sometimes, despite the need to be quiet at night, evenings were also times for silliness. One evening, for instance, Anne and Peter dressed up—he in his mother's dress, Anne in Peter's suit—and performed a skit. With her outgoing personality and love of attention, Anne was a natural performer. She was a good mimic, of everything from her cat's meow to her teacher's voice, and she loved having audiences for such performances.

These shows helped break up the monotony and tension of living in close quarters. However, there could never be any late-night entertainment. Between 9:00 and 10:00 each night, the people in the annex made preparations for sleep. This involved chores such as rearranging tables and chairs to make way for beds. Ten o'clock was bedtime.

More Routine

Weekends, rest days for most people, were devoted to noisy chores. The people in the annex aired out mattresses, beat rugs, did laundry, and otherwise cleaned house. Anne noted, "What happens in other people's houses during the rest of the

A Guide to Annex Life

The residents of the annex invented a tongue-in-cheek list of rules for life there, which they presented to Albert Pfeffer when he moved in. Anne reprinted them in her diary:

PROSPECTUS AND GUIDE TO THE SECRET ANNEX. . . .

Open all year round: Located in beautiful, quiet, wooded surroundings in the heart of Amsterdam. . . .

Price: Free.

Diet: Low-fat.

Running water in the bathroom (sorry, no bath) and on various inside and outside walls.

Cozy wood stoves for heating. . . .

Private radio with a direct line to London, New York, Tel Aviv and many other stations. Available to all residents after 6 P.M. . . .

Rest hours: From 10 P.M. to 7:30 A.M.; 10:15 A.M. on Sundays. Owing to circumstances, residents are required to observe rest hours during the daytime when instructed to do so by the Managements.

Use of language: It is necessary to speak softly at all times. Only the language of civilized people may be spoken, thus no German.

Reading and relaxation: No German books may be read, except for the classics and works of a scholarly nature. Other books are optional.

Calisthenics: Daily.

Singing: Only softly, and after 6 P.M. . . .

Baths: The washtub is available to all residents after 9 A.M. on Sundays. Residents may bathe in the bathroom, kitchen, private office or front office, as they choose.

week happens on Sundays here in the Secret Annex."[28]

Weekends were also times for baths, using a portable washtub and hot water from the office kitchen. Everybody had preferences about this ritual. Anne and Margot, for instance, liked to use the office for their baths. Anne wrote, "Since the curtains are drawn on Saturday afternoon, we scrub ourselves in the dark, while the one who isn't in the bath looks out the window through a chink in the curtains and gazes in wonder at the endlessly amusing people."[29]

One regular part of the annex's daily routine came from outside; chimes rang every quarter hour, day and night, from the nearby Westerkerk (Western Church), a beloved landmark that today is still one of the highest buildings in Amsterdam. The chimes bothered everyone except Anne, who saw them as a link to the outside world of freedom and found them reassuring. When the chimes temporarily stopped in 1943, probably because of a power failure, she remained anxious until they began again.

London Calling

In the evenings, the annex connected to the outside world in another way. On the radio in Otto's office, they heard nightly broadcasts, in Dutch, from the British Broadcasting Corporation (BBC) in London. Called *Radio Oranje*, in honor of the symbolic color of Dutch royalty, these programs were heard regularly by virtually every Dutch citizen, but in secret,

since the Nazis punished anyone caught listening.

The programs provided reliable news about the war. Newspapers were unreliable and heavily censored, with the news slanted to favor the Germans. Newspapers could not be relied on for factual coverage. The BBC broadcasts were the only way to form an accurate picture of the war's progress.

The broadcasts also helped the people in the annex understand the sounds of warfare. They could hear airplanes flying over Amsterdam every night on their way to bomb German targets, and they could hear other closer forms of warfare. Writer Ernst Schnabel comments, "Sometimes the house groaned and shook from the salvos [shots] of the anti-aircraft batteries."[30]

Just as important to Dutch listeners were the programs' messages of encouragement and hope. In particular, the affirmations of the Netherlands' beloved Queen Wilhelmina, who was exiled in London, lifted everyone's spirits. Miep Gies recalls, "We were like thirsty children, drinking every word spoken in these faraway broadcasts."[31]

Being Sick

They lived in fear of many things, one of the worst being the constant dread of illness. Little medicine was available, and there was no chance of seeing a doctor. Even a simple cold was a mortal danger, since a single ill-timed sneeze might have betrayed them all. Anne described in her diary a case of the flu: "With every cough, I had to duck under the blanket—once, twice, three times—and try to keep from coughing anymore."[32]

Anne, always frail, was especially vulnerable to colds and flu, as were Margot and Mrs. van Pels. Albert Pfeffer, a dentist, tried to maintain everyone's teeth, but he had virtually no instruments; he was forced to use brandy as an anaesthetic and cologne as a disinfectant.

Another of Anne's health problems arose from the long hours she spent reading and writing in dim light. Her eyesight became noticeably worse, and she complained of headaches. Clearly, she needed glasses. The group debated the wisdom of Anne's sneaking out to an optician, but decided that the risk was too great.

Hitler walks through the rubble after an Allied bombing raid. The Franks often heard Allied bombers on their way to strike Nazi targets.

Near Misses

Despite their precautions, the people in the annex came close to being discovered on several occasions. Early in 1943, for instance, 263 Prinsengracht was sold. The new owner arrived unexpectedly and asked Johannes Kleiman, Victor Kugler's second-in-command in the office, to show him around. Kleiman convinced the new owner that he did not have the key to the passageway leading to the annex, and the owner, satisfied he had seen enough, never came back.

On several occasions, burglars broke into the warehouse. Break-ins were not necessarily a threat; chances are that burglars would not

The Attic

In this passage from Anne Frank Remembered, *Miep Gies describes the one area of the annex that provided even a little bit of privacy and space:*

The only breath of fresh air could be had in the attic, where there was a skylight that opened and showed a patch of sky and the tower of the Westerkerk [Western Church]. Up in the attic the laundry was hung to dry; sacks of food stood out of the way, along with old file boxes from the office. Peter liked to tinker with his tools in the attic, and had made a little workshop. Anne and Margot liked to go upstairs to the attic to read.

have revealed their own crimes by reporting other suspicious activity. Police investigations into those burglaries, however, were genuine threats. One time, police checking out a break-in came so close that they rattled the door leading to the passageway connected to the annex.

After this terrifying moment, the van Pelses, panicked, lobbied for getting rid of the radio that was in Otto's office. They worried that it might be accidentally left on the forbidden BBC channel; if this were to be discovered, a full-scale search would no doubt take place. The worried van Pelses even suggested burning Anne's diary; if the annex were to be raided everyone would, of course, be found, but the diary would also alert the Nazis to the helpers' identities. Anne was horrified, but fortunately her beloved diary was not destroyed.

Losing Money

On another occasion, Hermann van Pels dropped his wallet in the warehouse.

Willem van Maaren, who had taken over as warehouse foreman after Johannes Voskuijl fell ill, found it. He took the wallet to Victor Kugler, minus the money it had contained. Van Maaren demanded to know whose it was, but Kugler professed ignorance. This event was a real disaster. Not only were the foreman's suspicions aroused, but the van Pels family also lost some of its precious cash.

The question of money became increasingly serious as the months dragged on. Even the Franks, who were better off financially than the van Pelses, were forced to sell jewelry and other valuables on Amsterdam's black market, using their helpers as agents.

The helpers also found other ways to make money for their friends. Kugler, for instance, sold spices without recording the sales. The income went to cover some of the *onderduiker*'s expenses, which were varied. As Otto recalled in 1971, "Along with food, we needed many other things as well, of course: toilet articles, medicine,

... books, and other things to keep us busy."[33]

The Annex Diet

Some things were not in short supply. For instance, they had plenty of canned food and dried beans and peas (though beans sometimes had to be individually rubbed to remove mold). Finding bread, milk, and fresh fruit and vegetables was another matter.

With food in short supply everywhere, what could be found was erratic. Miep recalls, "Sometimes now when I went shopping I would find the shops half-empty. The Germans had begun to take our food and ship it to their Fatherland [Germany].... It was not unusual to wait in a long line at a shop, finally get to the counter, and find that there was almost nothing to buy: a few beans, some wilted lettuce, half-rotted potatoes."[34]

Sometimes, what was available was delicious. In the summer of 1944, for instance, a large supply of strawberries arrived in the office. Many were smuggled upstairs for jam-making or immediate consumption. Anne wrote, "We ate

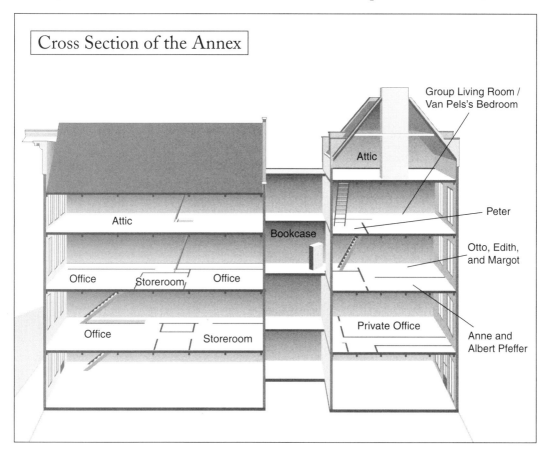

Cross Section of the Annex

Group Living Room / Van Pels's Bedroom

Attic

Attic

Bookcase

Peter

Office   Storeroom   Office

Otto, Edith, and Margot

Office   Storeroom

Private Office

Anne and Albert Pfeffer

hot cereal with strawberries, buttermilk with strawberries, bread with strawberries, strawberries for dessert, strawberries with sugar, strawberries with sand. For two days there was nothing but strawberries, strawberries, strawberries, and then our supply was either exhausted or in jars, safely under lock and key."[35]

Most of the time, however, the annex dwellers ate poorly. In the spring of 1943, Anne noted, "Our food is terrible. Breakfast consists of plain, unbuttered bread and ersatz [imitation] coffee. For the last two weeks lunch has been either spinach or cooked lettuce with huge potatoes that have a rotten, sweetish taste. If you're trying to diet, the Annex is the place to be!"[36]

Scrounging

The helpers had various methods to find food for the annex. For instance, Jan Gies got extra ration coupons (used for staples such as bread and milk) through his connections in the anti-Nazi underground. Bep and Miep received extra food from local shopkeepers, who knew that the women were buying unusually large amounts, but who also asked no questions. And Kleiman had a baker friend who supplied bread without requiring coupons, saying he could be repaid after the war. (After the war, the baker forgave the debt completely.)

Somehow, the helpers also found treats whenever there was a birthday or a holiday. These were often nothing more than a little extra butter or sugar, but even such a humble gift meant the *onderduikers* could enjoy a cake.

Occasionally, Anne and the others were able to repay the helpers' kindness. On Miep's thirty-fifth birthday, the van

The Bean Disaster

Sometimes, life in the annex had moments of comedy. One involved the many sacks of beans they kept stored. One day, while Peter was moving a sack upstairs to the attic and Anne stood in the stairway below him, the bag's seam broke and a shower of hard brown beans poured out. Of this, as quoted by van der Rol and Verhoeven in *Anne Frank: Beyond the Diary: A Photographic Remembrance*, Anne wrote, "There were about fifty pounds in that sack and the noise was enough to waken the dead. Downstairs they thought the old house with all its contents was coming down on them."

She and Peter froze in terror. Fortunately, no one was in the warehouse or offices below, and after the panic passed they could laugh about it. Anne and Peter were able to pick up most of the beans, although for days afterward everyone was still finding the little items in various corners of the stairway.

Pelses gave her an antique ring from their jewelry stash, although they could have sold it. One Christmas, knowing that Miep had a sweet tooth, Anne saved up her rations and made a precious batch of candies. Anne made Miep taste them right away, in order to see the blissful look on her face.

Observing Hanukkah

The Franks, who were not strictly observant Jews, nonetheless honored the religion's holidays. Even in the annex they celebrated Hanukkah.

Hanukkah commemorates an ancient battle between the Syrians and a group of Jews called the Maccabees. After the battle, one night's worth of oil for the eternal holy light in the temple of Jerusalem miraculously lasted eight days, until a fresh supply could arrive. Hanukkah marks this occasion by lighting successively larger numbers of candles for eight days.

However, just as in ancient times, the people in the annex did not have enough fuel. They could not afford to burn all of the candles used in a traditional Hanukkah observance. Instead, they sang holiday songs and burned candles for just ten minutes on one evening, using a menorah (a ritual candelabra) that Mr. van Pels had made.

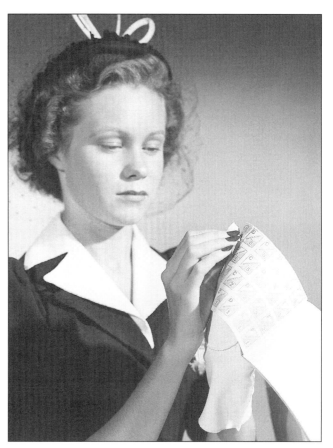

Jan Gies bought ration coupons like these on the black market to help supply the annex with food.

Future Plans

All through the years they stayed hidden, the people in the annex discussed what they would do when the war ended. They had reason to believe this would happen soon; it had been a long and brutal fight, but a victory against Hitler seemed inevitable. On June 6, 1944, known as D Day, the Allied (British and American) forces crossed the English Channel to France for a final push. From then on, liberation from the Nazis seemed close at hand.

Acknowledging the Helpers

In this passage from her diary entry of January 1944 (Definitive Edition), Anne acknowledges the hard work and sacrifices of Miep and the others who aided the annex dwellers:

There are many resistance groups, such as Free Netherlands, that forge identity cards, provide financial support to those in hiding, organize hiding places and find work for young Christians who go underground. It's amazing how much these generous and unselfish people do, risking their own lives to help and save others.

The best example of this is our own helpers, who have managed to pull us through so far and will hopefully bring us safely to shore. . . . Never have they uttered a single word about the burden we must be, never have they complained that we're too much trouble.

They come upstairs every day and talk to the men about business and politics, to the women about food and wartime difficulties and to the children about books and newspapers. They put on their most cheerful expressions, bring flowers and gifts for birthdays and holidays and are always ready to do what they can. That's something we should never forget; while others display their heroism in battle or against the Germans, our helpers prove theirs every day by their good spirits and affection.

Margot and Mr. van Pels both said the first thing they wanted in the outside world was a bath in a real bathtub. Mrs. van Pels yearned for cream-filled cakes, while Edith wanted a cup of real coffee. Peter planned to see a movie; Pfeffer wanted to reunite with his sweetheart; and Otto hoped to visit Bep's ill father and his own family members.

Anne's daydreams included a home for her family and school. She missed the guidance of her teachers and the companionship of her classmates. As for her plans as an adult, however, she had no desire to settle down; she wanted to travel the world as a journalist. In preparation for this, she began to write seriously.

Chapter Four

Keeping the Diary

The first entries in Anne's diary were sporadic. Within two months of her enforced hiding, however, she was making long, regular entries. The diary became, among other things, Anne's primary instrument in training herself to be a journalist. These self-taught lessons made her increasingly confident over time in her abilities as a writer. Writers Alfred Kazin and Anne Birstein note, "From the very first it was more to her than a purely personal record of triumphs and defeats. . . . An uncanny sense of an unseen audience, actually of posterity, prevails throughout her work."[37]

By April 1944, Anne was able to make an observation that sounds only a little doubtful about her writing abilities: I finally realized that I must do my schoolwork to keep from being ignorant, to get on in life, to become a journalist, because that's what I want! I know I can write. A few of my stories are good, my descriptions of the Secret Annex are humorous, much of my diary is vivid and alive, but . . . it remains to be seen whether I really have talent.[38]

Anne apparently realized the significance of her little diary, both to herself and to the world at large, right from the beginning. Her diary had been the first thing that she packed into her schoolbag on that hectic final evening at home. Although she could not have guessed its true importance, it was as if she already suspected what an important role the diary would play in her life.

How She Wrote
Anne wrote in her diary on a regular basis.

Thinking of Others

The earliest entries in Anne's diaries are self-absorbed in ways typical of adolescence. However, as she matured, her feelings became gradually more outward looking, as shows this entry from November 1942 (Definitive Edition):

We're so fortunate here, away from the turmoil. We wouldn't have to give a moment's thought to all this suffering if it weren't for the fact that we're so worried about those we hold dear, whom we can no longer help. I feel wicked sleeping in a warm bed, while somewhere out there my dearest friends are dropping from exhaustion or being knocked to the ground.

Nearly every day, when her studies and chores were finished, Anne found a private spot and wrote. Not surprisingly, considering the annex's crowded conditions, she almost always had trouble finding a secluded location. If Pfeffer was not in their shared bedroom, Anne could use the desk there. However, that was not often the case. Use of their shared desk, in fact, was a continual source of contention between the two. Pfeffer felt that, as an adult, he had priority; he scorned Anne's writing as child's play, insisting that his Spanish studies were more important. Otto stepped in as a peacemaker, creating a schedule that allowed Pfeffer and Anne to share the desk. However, at least according to Anne, the schedule still favored Pfeffer. Frequently, she retreated instead to the attic.

She wrote with a fountain pen that her grandmother in Aachen had given her on her ninth birthday. When she was not using her diary, Anne stored it in her father's old leather briefcase.

Soon, she filled the diary and had to move on to new volumes. Miep was able to scrounge extra paper—first a blank school notebook, then empty ledger books from the office, and, finally, loose sheets of office paper. Any kind of paper was scarce, and Anne carefully treasured each bit Miep brought her.

Revising the Diary

Sometime in the spring of 1944, as she continued to add to her diary, Anne began copying and revising her early entries. Her idea was to make the writing suitable for a wide audience, either as journalism or a novel.

This task was inspired by a *Radio Oranje* broadcast she heard on March 28, 1944. Gerrit Bolkestein, the exiled Dutch minister of education and culture, commented that evening that diaries of life in the wartime Netherlands would be interesting and valuable documents. He said:

If our descendants are to understand fully what we as a nation have had to endure and overcome during these years, then what we really need are ordinary documents—a diary, letters from a worker in Germany, a collection of sermons given by a parson or a priest. Not until we succeed in bringing together vast quantities of this simple, everyday material will the picture of our struggle for freedom be painted in its full depth and glory.[39]

Anne immediately set about revising her diary. She was never sure whether her new version would become nonfiction, in the form of a memoir, or fiction, in the form of a novel. However, she liked the idea of a novel, which she wanted to call *The Secret Annex*. She commented, "Just imagine how interesting it would be if I were to publish a novel about the Secret Annex. The title alone would make people think it was a detective story. Seriously, though, ten years after the war people would find it very amusing to read how we lived, what we ate and what we talked about as Jews in hiding."[40]

Changing Names and Events

As she revised her diary, Anne also decided to draw up a list of pseudonyms to use for the people in the annex, as well as for their helpers. This was an attempt to make her writing more novelistic, and also a way to hide the identities of real people who would have been in danger if the diary were ever found.

Thus, Victor Kugler and Johannes Kleiman became Harry Kraler and Simon Koophuis. Hermann, Auguste, and Peter van Pels were called Hans, Petronella, and Alfred van Daan. Albert Pfeffer became Albert Dussel. Bep Voskuijl was referred

Anne Frank wrote in her diary regularly and revised early entries to make them suitable for publication.

to as Elli Vossen, and Miep Gies was Miep van Santen; her boyfriend Jan was called Henk van Santen. Anne referred to her own family as Frederik and Nora Robin and their daughters, Betty and Anne Robin. (Some of these false names were kept, others changed slightly, when the diary was first published.)

The aspiring fiction writer also did not hesitate to change real events if it suited her novelistic purposes. Anne edited her original entries rather liberally to make them sound more like plausible fiction. Melissa Müller notes, "If she didn't like the original text anymore, she went at it like a stage director, changing sequences of events and reformulating entire passages."[41]

At the same time that she wrote her straight journal entries, Anne also worked on other kinds of writing. Among these were essays based on her memories from before the war, short stories, and fables about such imaginative things as dwarfs and elves. (These writings have since been published under the title *Anne Frank's Tales from the Secret Annex.*)

On several occasions, Anne asked Johannes Kleiman to send her writing to newspapers under a pseudonym. He refused, however, because he thought that the risk of discovery would be too great. In any case, these other kinds of writing never kept Anne from concentrating on her primary focus, her diary.

A Natural Writer

In this passage from Anne Frank: The Biography, *Melissa Müller comments on Anne's developing writing style:*

The pleasure Anne took in writing was evident even in her first entries. . . . Each month, her choice of words became more colorful, her style more sure and elegant, her descriptions and interpretations more subtle and sophisticated. She was idealistic but not naïve.

Her style improved rapidly, with astonishing speed considering her age. But even when she began experimenting with language, her sentences were never artificial. She [always wrote] in a precise, confident, economical style stunning in its honesty.

Although very little was happening in Anne's life—or perhaps because of that—she always had something new to report. The more she wrote, the sharper her observations became and the clearer her expression of those observations; the keener, too, her understanding of others and—as if she could step outside herself and look back in—of herself as well.

Margot and Her Parents' Bedroom

Recording Her Feelings

Anne had begun her diary purely for herself, and many of the entries were highly personal. They reflected the sudden mood shifts and dramatic emotions that adolescents commonly experience, such as the need for independence, conflicts with parents, and a developing awareness of sexuality.

Unlike most adolescents, however, Anne was not able to express her emotions in normal ways. She had no way to let off steam when she was angry. She could not talk to others who were having the same feelings (Margot and Peter were so different from her that Anne had difficulty confiding in them). She could not take a long walk or even slam a door.

And, of course, there was no question of running away, or even finding more than a brief period of solitude away from prying eyes. For one thing, the young people in the annex were subject to constant surveillance and criticism by the adults. Perhaps this was not difficult for Margot and Peter; both of them seemed able to bear confinement and scrutiny more easily, or at least quietly.

Not so with Anne, who was far more volatile and animated. She desperately needed a way to vent her emotions. And, since she could not speak as freely as she would have liked without drawing criticism,

Changing Moods

Many of the entries in Anne's diary concern her feelings toward her family, which could veer from one extreme to the other depending on her mood and circumstances. Here are three representative excerpts from the Definitive Edition:

> I finally told Daddy that I love "him" more than I do Mother, to which he replied that it was just a passing phase, but I don't think so. I simply can't stand Mother, and I have to force myself not to snap at her all the time, and to stay calm, when I'd rather slap her across the face. . . . I can imagine Mother dying someday, but Daddy's death seems inconceivable. It's very mean of me, but that's how I feel. I hope Mother will never read this or anything else I've written.

even about mundane things, she turned to her diary. Writing long letters to "my dearest Kitty" helped quench Anne's deep need to express her feelings.

Criticism

One recurring theme in Anne's diary concerns the frustration and anger she felt over her relationship with her mother. Anne adored her father, whom she affectionately called Pim, and they generally were close. However, Anne's mother frequently seemed unsympathetic and critical, and the two often argued. Forced confinement in the annex meant that fights often erupted over trivial matters that otherwise would have been ignored. Otto frequently needed to step in as peacemaker between the two.

Many of Anne's diary entries also chronicle criticisms directed toward her by Mr. and Mrs. van Pels. Mrs. van Pels,

in particular, was a highly strung woman who felt that the strong-minded Anne was not being disciplined enough. In recording such conversations and her own outraged reactions to them, Anne recognized that her diary was replacing the typical forms of expression open to most people. She noted in her diary that her violent outbursts on paper were simply expressions of anger that she normally would have taken care of by stamping her foot or calling her mother names behind her back.

Describing the Others

Anne did not simply record her moods and thoughts in her diary, however. She also made detailed descriptions of life in the annex, and of those who shared it with her. These observations were often cuttingly sharp, unfavorable, and unsparing. For instance, she noted that Mrs. van Pels was nervous and subject to periodic fits of hysterics, convinced that the Nazis were about to descend at any moment. She was alternately frantic and despondent, Anne wrote, and even threatened suicide on occasion.

Interpersonal relationships were another subject for Anne. It was inevitable that tempers frequently flared in the annex, with people living in such close quarters and under such tension. Anne was able to describe in her diary the quarrels that developed, over seemingly trivial matters, in such intimate surroundings.

One long-running antagonism was the war between Albert Pfeffer and Anne herself, who continued to irritate each other at every turn. Anne described in her diary such incidents as the battle over the use of the desk in their room and his obnoxious habit of waking her up by doing his daily exercises. She suspected

that he hoarded food without sharing. She also described his habit of retreating to the toilet to read for hours whenever the Franks and the van Pelses were having a disagreement; as the only single adult, Pfeffer found himself the odd man out at such times.

Peter van Pels, meanwhile, was dismissed by Anne early on in their confinement as an uninteresting and unpromising character. She wrote that he was "a soft, shy, gawky youth; can't expect much from his company."[42]

Falling in Love

Anne's low opinion of Peter changed over time, however. In fact, she revealed in her diary early in 1944 that she was starting to fall in love with Peter, whom Miep described as "a good-looking, stocky boy with thick dark hair, dreamy eyes, and a sweet nature."[43]

Dining Room

Anne had already had several male admirers. Her first serious boyfriend, in the months before she went into hiding, had been Helmuth Silberberg, a slightly older boy who was, like Anne, a German Jew. She had also developed a crush on another boy, Peter Schiff, but he did not reciprocate her affection.

However, not until quite late in their confinement together in the annex did Anne and Peter van Pels show any interest in each other. Peter, who was two years older than Anne and a year younger than Margot, had been too shy to become close to either. Margot and Anne, for their part, had not tried to further the friendship.

Then, in January 1944, Anne had a powerful dream about Peter Schiff, the object of her long-ago crush. She described in her diary how Peter's eyes suddenly met hers in the dream, and how she stared into them for a long time.

Anne realized that she had developed strong romantic feelings for Peter Schiff. She noted, "I simply have to go on living and praying to God that, if we ever get out of here, Peter's path will cross mine and he'll gaze into my eyes, read the love in them and say, 'Oh, Anne, if I'd only known, I'd have come to you long ago.'"[44]

Since that Peter was not present, however, Anne began to turn her attentions toward the other one. She wrote, "My longing to talk to someone has become so intense that somehow or other I took it into my head to choose Peter [van Pels]."[45]

Peter's Bedroom

In the face of these attentions, Peter himself gradually became attracted to Anne and slowly overcame his shyness. That spring, under the watchful eyes of the adults, the two teens developed strong crushes on each another. Anne wrote extensively about these feelings: "I feel as if I were about to explode. . . . I walk from one room to another, breathe through a crack in the window frame. . . . I think spring is inside me."[46]

Attic Dates

Of course, Anne and Peter could not go out together like normal teens. Instead of a regular date, the best they could manage was a trip to the attic. When the sun was shining through the single skylight there, they would sit on the floor and pretend they were at the beach.

Much of Anne Frank's diary explores the tense relationship she shared with her mother Edith.

They would look at the tiny patch of blue sky and the lone visible chestnut tree, watch seagulls and other birds flying by, and try to catch a breath of fresh air. Anne, by far the more forthcoming of the two, usually initiated their conversations, which she often turned to such frank subjects as puberty and sex.

Anne's tender feelings about Peter van Pels quickly turned into a desire to link her life to his. By March she was writing, "I [have] discovered an inner happiness underneath my superficial and cheerful exterior. . . . Now I live only for Peter, since what happens to me in the future depends largely on him!"[47]

Not until the following month, however, did they grow bold enough to share a kiss. About this Anne wrote, "Oh, it was so wonderful. I could hardly talk, my pleasure was so intense; he caressed my cheek and arm, a bit clumsily."[48] Within days, she was delightedly reporting a mutual kiss "near" the mouth.

Anne Frank developed a close relationship with Peter van Pels (pictured) and the two often pretended to go on dates together.

meant that there was always a certain amount of excitement in Anne's life. She noted, "I am young and strong and am living a great adventure; I am still in the midst of it and can't grumble the whole day long."[49]

Nonetheless, it could not be denied that life in the annex was often crushingly dull, with the same routines performed by the same people every day. Sometimes, Anne used her diary to express how frustrating this could be. At one especially low point she wrote, "Dearest Kitty, this morning I was wondering whether you ever felt like a cow, having to chew my stale news over and over again until you're so fed up with the monotonous fare that you yawn and secretly wish Anne would dig up something new."[50]

At other times, Anne revealed in her diary the toll that the daily ration of fear was taking on her and the group as a whole. In one entry, she noted, "One day we're laughing at the comical side of life in hiding, and the next day (and there are many such days), we're frightened, and the fear, tension, and despair can be read on our faces." On another

Boredom, Despair, Hope

Emotional dramas such as Anne's slowly developing relationship with Peter, and the constant fear that everyone lived with, occasion she wrote, "We've almost forgotten how to laugh. Sometimes I'm afraid my face is going to sag with all this sorrow and that my mouth is going to permanently droop at the corners. The others aren't doing any better."[51]

The last entry in Anne's diary is dated Tuesday, August 1, 1944. In it, she discusses some of the confusing emotions she had been experiencing. She ends it with the hope that she can "keep trying to find a way to become what I'd like to be and what I could be if . . . if only there were no other people in the world."[52]

There are no more diary entries. Three days after her final entry, everyone in the annex was discovered and taken away. After slightly more than two years, Anne's confinement was over.

Chapter Five

DISCOVERED AND DEPORTED

Throughout their enforced confinement, Anne and the others in the annex had managed to maintain a considerable amount of optimism about the future. After all, they had successfully remained hidden in the middle of an occupied city. Furthermore, judging by the news on the radio, the Allies were making steady progress toward freeing the occupied countries of Europe. The end of the war was clearly coming closer every day.

However, Anne was also aware that the danger was not over. The threat of discovery remained real and constant. In a diary entry from late in 1943, she expressed her fear over this by imagining herself and the seven others in a steadily tightening trap: "I see the eight of us with our 'Secret Annexe' as if we were a little piece of blue heaven, surrounded by heavy black rain clouds. The round, clearly defined spot where we stand is still safe, but the clouds gather more closely about us and the circle which separates us from the approaching danger closes more and more tightly."[53]

And so, when the Gestapo appeared at 263 Prinsengracht on the morning of Friday, August 4, 1944, it was not a complete surprise. For many months, the raid had been dreaded but not unexpected.

The Arrest

That morning, Gestapo Department IV B4, the division of the police in charge of rounding up Jews, received a phone call at its office on Amsterdam's Euterpestraat. The voice on the other end informed the Nazis that several Jews were hiding at 263 Prinsengracht. The voice of the anonymous informant was Dutch. According to some reports, it was a woman.

A group of four was sent immediately from the Euterpestraat office. The unit was composed of three Dutch civilians and a leader, Karl Josef Silberbauer, an Austrian-born sergeant in the *Schutzstaffel*, or SS, the primary branch of the Nazi military police force.

The group stormed into the office at about 10:30 that morning and told Johannes Kleiman and Victor Kugler that they knew Jews were hidden in the building. Miep Gies and Bep Voskuijl were told to stay quiet and in their places. The police seemed to know already about the hidden doorway and they forced Kugler to take them to it.

Clattering up the steep stairs into the annex, the first person the Nazis saw was Edith Frank, who was in her room. Edith was too shocked to scream. The other *onderduikers* were engaged in various activities elsewhere in the annex; Otto and Peter were upstairs in Peter's room, where Otto was correcting the young man's English lessons.

The police quickly rounded up everyone. They were all as shocked and silent as Edith. No one yelled or tried to resist, although Margot began crying quietly.

Sergeant Silberbauer informed the *onderduikers* that they were under arrest and were to pack their clothes immediately. Since everyone had kept knapsacks handy in case of an emergency, such as a

The Nazis Arrive

Many years after the fact, Victor Kugler, one of the Franks' helpers, described their arrest. His recollections are reprinted in Harry Paape's "The Arrest," in Anne Frank: Reflections on Her Life and Legacy:

Suddenly a staff-sergeant of the [Nazi] "Green Police" and three Dutch civilians entered my office and . . . said to me, we want the person who is in charge here. That is myself, I replied. Then, "Come along," they ordered. [After] the sergeant had looked at everything, he went out in the corridor, ordering me again to come along. At the end of the corridor they drew their revolvers all at once and the sergeant ordered me to push aside the bookcase at the head of the corridor and to open the door behind it.

I said: "But there's only a bookcase there!" At that he turned nasty, for he knew everything. He took hold of the bookcase and pulled at it; it yielded and the secret door was exposed. . . . They opened the door, and I had to precede them up the steps. The policemen followed me; I could feel their pistols in my back.

Nazi soldiers arrest Jewish factory workers in 1943. Tipped off by an anonymous informant, Nazi soldiers arrested the annex occupants on the morning of August 4, 1944.

natural disaster, there was little packing to do. Otto recalled, "They gave us more time than we needed. We all knew what we had to pack—the same belongings we had planned on taking in case of fire."[54]

Ransacking the Annex

Silberbauer and the other Nazis searched the annex carefully for loot. This was standard procedure; all valuable items belonging to arrested Jews were taken either for the army or for use back in Germany.

Historian Martin Gilbert comments, "Loot was a central element in the Nazi persecution of the Jews. The murder of six million people provided a source of rich booty for the SS, for the German war machine and for Germans generally."[55]

Now, from the annex, the Nazis took money, silverware, the menorah that Hermann van Pels had made, and other valuables. Silberbauer looked inside Otto's briefcase, hoping to find something worth taking. When he shook out the contents, however, he saw nothing but what seemed to be worthless notebooks and papers.

The officer kept the briefcase, using it to carry silverware he had found. The papers that had been in the briefcase, Anne's diary and other writings, were stepped on and ignored in the chaos of the raid.

At one point, Silberbauer saw Otto's metal footlocker, which dated from his days in the German army during World War I. Otto's name and officer's rank were clearly stenciled on it. Otto had been a lieutenant, a higher rank than that of the Nazi sergeant who was arresting him.

Taken Away

Silberbauer was taken aback and puzzled; why, he wondered aloud, had Otto not registered as a war veteran? Doing so would not have saved him from deportation; but it would, at least, have given him the privilege of being sent to Theresienstadt, a concentration camp in what is now the Czech Republic. But Otto had not done so because it would have separated him from his family. Theresienstadt had a reputation for being more humane than the other camps; Otto wryly recalled later of his captor, "Apparently he thought Theresienstadt [was] a rest camp."[56]

The End

Janny Brandes-Brillesliper was perhaps the last person to see Anne Frank alive, and after her liberation she became the one who officially notified Otto Frank of Anne's and Margot's deaths. In this excerpt from an oral history in Willy Lindwer's The Last Seven Months of Anne Frank, *she describes their tragic ends:*

At a certain moment in the final days, Anne stood in front of me, wrapped in a blanket. She didn't have any more tears. Oh, we hadn't had tears for a long time. And she told me that she had such a horror of the lice and fleas in her clothes and that she had thrown all of her clothes away. It was the middle of winter and she was wrapped in one blanket. I gathered up everything I could find to give her so that she was dressed again. We didn't have much to eat, and Lientje [Janny's sister] was terribly sick but I gave Anne some of our bread ration.

Terrible things happened. Two days later, I went to look for the girls. Both of them were dead!

First, Margot had fallen out of bed onto the stone floor. She couldn't get up anymore. Anne died a day later. We had lost all sense of time. It is possible that Anne lived a day longer.

While the raid was going on, Jan Gies came to the office, to have lunch with Miep as usual. She hurriedly told him that the Gestapo were there, and that he needed to leave immediately. He had close ties with the Dutch underground resistance, and it would have been very dangerous for him to come into contact with the police.

She quickly handed him extra ration cards and other evidence. He took them back to his own office and emptied his pockets of any other incriminating evidence. Then he returned, standing on the other side of the canal from 263 Prinsengracht to watch helplessly as the Jews were led away.

The prisoners were led down the staircase and into a waiting truck. The whole time, they remained as eerily calm as when the raid had begun. Perhaps they were simply too shocked and dispirited to yell or cry out. Miep Gies recalled that she listened to it all from her desk in the office, where she had been told to stay: "I could tell from their footsteps that they were coming down like beaten dogs."[57]

Janny Brandes-Brilleslijper, a fellow prisoner at Bergen-Belsen, was the last person known to have seen Anne Frank alive.

Taken Away

The two secretaries, Miep and Bep, were questioned but not arrested. However, the police did arrest Kugler and Kleiman. They were taken, along with the eight people from the annex, to the Gestapo headquarters, where everyone was put in a room together. Otto Frank later recalled that he expressed his deep sorrow that these men had been arrested simply for

A Celebration

Lin Jaldati, who, with her sister, was in the Bergen-Belsen camp with Anne and Margot Frank, describes easing some of the hardships there with a makeshift celebration. Her memories are reprinted in Anne Frank: Reflections on Her Life and Legacy:

One day in December we all got a few pieces of hard cheese and some marmalade. The SS and the matrons went off afternoons and celebrated. It was Christmas. With Margot and Anne Frank and the Daniels sisters we were three pairs of sisters. We wanted that night to celebrate St. Nicholas, Hanukkah, and Christmas in our own way. Jannie [her sister] had gotten to know a group of Hungarians, a few of whom worked in the SS kitchen. With their help she succeeded in getting two handfuls of potato peelings. . . . Anne gathered up a clove of garlic, the Daniels sisters found a beet and a carrot. I sang a few songs for the matrons [female guards] in another bunk and danced a Chopin waltz, singing the melody myself, for which I got a handful of sauerkraut. We saved a bit of bread from the rations, and each of us prepared a little surprise for the others. . . . So that's how we celebrated.

helping friends. Kugler replied, "Don't give it another thought. It was up to me, and I wouldn't have done it differently."[58]

Meanwhile, Miep and Bep remained in the office. When the two women, still in a state of shock, finally ventured up into the annex, they saw a huge mess. Miep recalled, "Right away, from the door, I saw that the place had been ransacked. Drawers were open, things strewn all over the floor. Everywhere objects were overturned. My eyes took in a scene of terrible pillage."[59]

The two picked up as many items as possible. These included books, Otto's typewriter, and Anne's diary and papers.

Miep had noticed, on the floor amidst the chaos of scattered possessions, Anne's little diary. Knowing how important the diary had always been to Anne, she enlisted Bep's help in gathering it up, along with handfuls of loose pages covered in Anne's handwriting.

Westerbork

The ten arrested individuals spent a few days at the Euterpestraat prison. Kugler and Kleiman were then sent to work camps. Meanwhile, the eight from the annex were taken by train to Westerbork, the transit camp for Dutch Jews.

For Anne and the others, the train journey to the eastern part of the Netherlands was one of fear and uncertainty, but also, paradoxically, one of relatively good spirits. Otto recalled, "We rode in a regular passenger train. The fact that the door was bolted did not matter very much to us. We were together again, and had been given a little food for the journey. We knew where we were bound, but in spite of that it was almost as if we were once more going traveling, or having an outing."[60]

Anne, especially, was almost cheerful; what she saw from the train fascinated her. After more than two years of seeing nothing but the same rooms and faces day after day, a train ride through farmland and villages—even one leading to a prison camp—had an element of the miraculous.

Westerbork was only a transit camp, not one designed for extermination. Still, it was bleak and barren, and life there was difficult. On arrival, prisoners were separated by gender and sent to overcrowded barracks holding as many as three hundred prisoners apiece.

The eight from the annex were given special punishments because they had been captured, rather than having voluntarily given themselves up. They were assigned to the worst barracks. Their clothes were taken from them, unlike other prisoners, and they were given identifying uniforms of blue overalls with red patches. They were also provided with ill-fitting wooden shoes that were torture to wear, especially during the hours they were made to stand every day for roll calls.

Finding Cheer Amid Deprivation

Prisoners at Westerbork were put to work starting at 5:00 each morning. Seasoned prisoners advised the new arrivals to work hard; the rumor was that, if they were good workers, they might stay at Westerbork instead of being transferred to a death camp.

Otto tried to arrange jobs in the prison kitchen for Anne and Margot, since kitchen work was relatively easy. However, this proved impossible. Another way the Nazis punished Jews who had been hiding was to give them the hardest jobs.

For Anne and her family, this meant breaking up old batteries and salvaging parts to make new ones. They had to break each battery apart with a small chisel, then remove the carbon rods inside, scrape a paste of ammonium chloride off, and put each part into separate boxes. It was filthy work, and there was almost nowhere to wash up. It was also highly toxic; chemicals from the batteries burned the workers' hands and lungs.

At least the prisoners were allowed to converse while they worked. Everyone usually stayed on light topics—how life would be after the war or pleasant memories from before. This was, in part, a reflection of the prisoners' deep need to use optimism as a survival tool. British historian Martin Gilbert writes, "The hope of all Jews . . . was to survive, to live through the time of torment, to stay alive until Hitler, Nazism and Germany

Women hard at work in Bergen-Belsen manage to smile for a photo. Despite the hardships they faced, many concentration camp prisoners maintained a sense of optimism.

were defeated. The Yiddish [a Germanic language spoken by many Jews around the world] verb *überleben* (to live through) had a powerful resonance in every ghetto and camp."[61]

To Auschwitz

Despite the hardships, Anne found moments of happiness at Westerbork. Her life had an element of freedom, compared to the annex. She could breathe fresh air and walk around. There were new people for her to meet and talk to. The newness of the situation helped Anne distract herself from the reality that she was scheduled to be transferred to the

death camp at Auschwitz. Otto Frank even later recalled that at times Anne seemed relaxed, almost cheerful.

Her time at Westerbork did not last long, however. On September 3, about a month after the Nazis discovered them, the eight people from the annex were loaded onto a train, as part of a group totaling about a thousand. German troops armed with guns and attack dogs supervised the transfer. Their destination was Auschwitz, in German-occupied Poland. They were the very last of nearly one hundred thousand Jews who were moved from Westerbork to the notorious death camp.

"Nothing . . . Is Left"

In March 1945, shortly after his release from Auschwitz, Otto Frank wrote a letter to his cousin Milly Stanfield from a refugee camp in Poland. It is excerpted in Carol Ann Lee's The Hidden Life of Otto Frank:

I hope that this letter may reach you giving you the news that I am living. It really is a wonder. . . . I do not know how many of my comrades . . . are still living. I don't believe there are many. . . . Of Edith and the children I know nothing. . . .

We were hiding for more than two years in Amsterdam and our friends cared for us, looking after our food and all our needs in spite of all dangers. Luckily I earned enough money in those years to pay our way, but now I am a beggar, having lost everything except life. Nothing of my household is left, not a photo, not a letter of my children, nothing, nothing, but I don't want to think what will happen later and if I shall be able to work again. There are as many in the same situation. . . .

How shall I find you all and all my old friends? I always was optimistic and I am still trying my best.

The prisoners were transported by cattle car, standing up and packed nearly to the point of suffocation. There were no windows or seats, and barely any ventilation or water. Each car had only one bucket for use as a toilet, so most prisoners defecated where they stood.

For the Nazis, this method of transport was ruthlessly practical, moving as many people as quickly and cheaply as possible. But it served another purpose: It also deprived the prisoners of even more dignity and sense of self-preservation, bringing them one notch closer to broken despair. Melissa Müller notes, "The Nazis understood how to strip people of their sense of self-worth. They knew how to bring people to the point at which they would just give up."[62]

In the Death Camp

Three days after it left Westerbork, the train arrived in Auschwitz. Anne and the others immediately noticed a sickly sweet odor pervading the camp. This was the smell of the crematorium, where massive numbers of bodies were burned. Some of the prisoners had succumbed to disease or starvation; others had died from the brutal medical experiments the Nazis conducted, or from the systematic use of deadly gas on large groups.

Over half of the new arrivals—549 people, including all 79 of the children under the age of fifteen—were gassed immediately upon their arrival. The stronger, older ones, including Anne and Margot, were allowed to live so that they could work, at least until they were too weak to continue. Then, according to the plan, they would be sent to the gas chambers.

Anne and Margot, along with all others who were kept alive, were tattooed with identification numbers on their arms. As in Westerbork, the women and men were separated into different parts of the camp. The women also had their heads shaved; the men had already had this done at Westerbork. The hair of the female prisoners was then sold to German textile firms for use in blankets, pipe insulation, and other textile uses.

Concentration Camps Throughout Europe

SWEDEN
LATVIA
DENMARK
Baltic Sea
Neuengamme
LITHUANIA
Sachsenhausen-Oranienburg
Bergen-Belsen
Ravensbrück
NETHERLANDS
EAST PRUSSIA
Stutthof
U.S.S.R.
GERMANY
POLAND
Treblinka
Chelmno
Gross-Rosen
Sobibor
BELGIUM
Majdanek
Mittelbaudora
Auschwitz-Birkenau
Belzec
Flossenbürg
Theresienstadt
CZECHOSLOVAKIA
Zweiler-Struthof
Mauthausen
FRANCE
SWITZERLAND
HUNGARY
ROMANIA
AUSTRIA
Dachau

Detention camps/Gestapo prisons
Large-scale labor camps
Large-scale extermination camps

ITALY
YUGOSLAVIA
Adriatic Sea
BULGARIA
Mediterranean Sea

Life in Auschwitz

Not much information has survived about Anne's time at Women's Block 29 in Auschwitz. Undoubtedly she was put to work, perhaps hauling stones or digging up rolls of sod. At night she, along with a thousand or more other women, slept in a building originally designed as a barn for fifty-two horses.

There were no mattresses. A few lucky souls had thin blankets. There was one cup for every five prisoners, and women wore nothing but gray sacks as dresses. Everyone was hungry and thirsty all the time.

Everyone was also infested with lice, despite weekly doses of insecticide, and the camp was infested with mites and bedbugs, whose bites were bad enough to create open sores. Anne's body became so infected, as did Margot's and perhaps also Edith's, that they were sent to an isolation ward. This was the so-called scabies block, an unlit barracks overrun with mice and rats.

Eyewitness recollections of Anne's reaction to Auschwitz are conflicting. Some remember Anne as quiet and introverted, weeping often and having difficulty coping. Others, however, say that she remained strong and courageous, and that she even managed to find extra rations of bread for herself, Margot, and Edith.

Moved Again

Anne and Margot did not remain at Auschwitz long. The Russian army was quickly advancing, and was only sixty miles away from the camp by October 1944. The Germans, sensing the end and wanting to eliminate evidence of the camps, decided to move some of their prisoners away from the impending liberation forces.

And so, less than two months after their arrival at Auschwitz, the Frank sisters were moved again. At the end of October, they, along with thousands of others, were sent to a camp in Germany called Bergen-Belsen. Edith and Otto Frank remained at Auschwitz.

On the journey, Anne and Margot spent more days packed into another horrifically overcrowded cattle car. They suffered from hunger, thirst, and the cold of the impending winter. Many prisoners died along the way.

The Frank sisters survived, but they were weak and nearly frozen when they arrived. Furthermore, for the first time in their lives, they were without their parents close at hand to help them. They were more alone than they had ever been.

Bergen-Belsen

Life at Bergen-Belsen was even more terrible than at Auschwitz. The food at Auschwitz had been poor, but at least it had been served regularly. The barracks at Auschwitz had been crowded and bug-infested, but they seemed almost clean compared to Bergen-Belsen.

At Bergen-Belsen, moreover, there was virtually no food, and no water except what could be melted from snow. The

Glimpsing Anne Near the End

Near the end of her life, Anne was reunited with her friend Hanneli Goslar at Bergen-Belsen. The two were in different parts of the camp, separated by barbed wire, and Hanneli put together a small package of food and clothes to throw to her friend. Her memories are excerpted in an oral history, "Her Last Days," in Anne Frank: Reflections on Her Life and Legacy:

We agreed to try to meet the next evening at eight o'clock—I believe I still had a watch. And, in fact, I succeeded in throwing the package over. But I heard her screaming, and I called out, "What happened?"

And Anne answered, "Oh, the woman standing next to me caught it, and she won't give it back to me." Then she began to scream.

I calmed her down a bit and said, "I'll try again but I don't know if I'll be able to." We arranged to meet again, two or three days later, and I was actually able to throw over another package. She caught it; that was the main thing.

After these three or four meetings at the barbed-wire fence in Bergen-Belsen, I didn't see her again, because the people in Anne's camp were transferred to another section in Bergen-Belsen. That happened around the end of February. That was the last time I saw Anne alive and spoke to her. During that time, my father died. . . . and I didn't go out for a few days. When I went to look for her again, I found that the section was empty.

shelters were filthy, and so overcrowded that at first Anne and Margot had to sleep in a huge tent with several hundred other women. There were no blankets or mattresses to protect them from the wintry ground. When a storm blew the tent down, Anne and Margot managed to find, inside a crowded, dirty barrack, a single bunk they could share.

Food, when there was any, consisted of fare such as bread made mostly of sawdust or soup containing mice, rags, or tufts of hair. Hundreds of people died every week of starvation and disease. Rats were everywhere, nibbling on the skin of those who had died in their bunks during the night and often attacking the living.

A Friend

Anne had one bright moment at Bergen-Belsen. She discovered that a childhood friend, Hanneli Goslar, was in another section of the camp. Hanneli, also called Hannah or Lies, had been there since early 1944, but as a so-called exchange Jew, a prisoner being held in case the

An elderly Hanneli Goslar recounts her interactions with childhood friend Anne Frank at Bergen-Belsen shortly before Frank's death.

Allies wanted to exchange prisoners of war with the Nazis.

Exchange Jews were assigned to somewhat less terrible barracks. They also received better treatment, such as the privilege of receiving food and clothes from the Red Cross. Despite such treatment, however, both of Hanneli's parents had died there.

When Hanneli heard that Anne and Margot Frank were at the camp, she went to the barbed-wire fence that separated her area from theirs and called out. Mrs. van Pels happened to hear her and took a message to Anne. Margot was ill and unable to come, but Hanneli and Anne were able to meet at night, separated by barbed wire.

Hanneli recalled later how shocked she was at Anne's condition. Anne had lost so much weight that she seemed like a ghost. She was sick, cold, and clearly starving to death. Hanneli recalled, "It was so terrible. She immediately began to cry, and she told me, 'I don't have any parents anymore.'"[63]

The End

In March 1945 Margot Frank died of typhus, a bacterial disease passed on by lice and other insects. Anne Frank, who was never informed of her sister's death, also died of typhus a few days later. The exact date is unknown.

The sisters were buried in mass graves. They were only two of the seventeen thousand people who died in Bergen-Belsen during the month of March alone. No one knows the precise number; the camp's besieged adminis-tration had long since stopped keeping close records.

Meanwhile, the Allies had liberated much of Europe. On April 15 a contingent of British soldiers freed the prisoners at Bergen-Belsen. At the end of April, facing certain defeat, Adolf Hitler committed suicide, and on May 7 the German army unconditionally surrendered. Anne's death thus came only weeks before the camp's liberation, less than two months before the end of the war, and just three months shy of her sixteenth birthday.

Chapter Six

SAVING THE DIARY

Nearly everyone else from the annex also died in the concentration camps. Hermann van Pels was killed in the gas chamber at Auschwitz in October or November 1944. Auguste van Pels was transported to Bergen-Belsen and then to Theresienstadt, where she died in April 1945.

Peter van Pels, sent to the Mauthausen camp in Austria, died there just before the camp's liberation. Albert Pfeffer was transported to the Neuengamme camp, where he died in December 1944. Edith Frank died of hunger and exhaustion in Auschwitz in January 1945.

Of the eight *onderduikers*, Otto Frank was the only survivor. Set free when the Russians liberated Auschwitz in January 1945, he was one of the forty-seven hundred Dutch Jews who lived to come back. Of those Dutch Jews deported by the Germans, fewer than one in twenty returned. Only about one-third of those who had gone into hiding had survived. And all the survivors lost virtually everything they had once owned.

Searching

Otto could not go home directly. He slowly made his way to Amsterdam via refugee camps in Russia, Poland, and France. Like all of the camp survivors, Otto was desperate to find his family. In March, while in Poland awaiting transportation, he wrote to his mother, "Where Edith and the children are, I do not know. We have been apart since 5 September 1944. I merely heard that they have been transported to Germany. One has to be hopeful, to see them back well and healthy."[64]

Otto did not learn for several months that Edith was dead. Even then, he still knew nothing about his daughters. At one point, Otto wrote to his sister Leni that he was not sure how he could ever go on living without the children, having already lost his wife.

The chaos of the war meant that this letter, along with others Otto wrote, took months to reach their destinations. Not until the end of May 1945 did Otto's relatives have any idea what had happened to him. When his mother found Otto, she wrote that she had initiated a search for Anne and Margot, but could do little more than offer consoling words: "To know that you are alone in your mourning for Edith and still without news of your beloved children is the most terrible experience I have had to bear in a life that has often been very hard."[65]

Searching

Otto finally arrived in Amsterdam in June 1945. Miep and Jan Gies invited him to stay with them, rent free. He tried to restart his business, and he searched for news of his daughters. Otto did this by placing ads in the newspapers, contacting known survivors of the camps, and scanning published lists of victims.

Miep Gies recollects that there seemed to be a reasonable chance they were still alive: "Mr. Frank held high hopes for the girls, because Bergen-Belsen was not a death camp. There were no gassings there. It was a work camp—filled with hunger and disease, but with no apparatus for liquidation."[66]

However, in July 1945, Otto received reliable word that his daughters were dead. Checking Red Cross lists of concentration camp victims and survivors, as he regularly did, he found their names, with crosses next to them indicating they had not survived. He searched out the person

"The Real Miracle"

Writers Ann Birstein and Alfred Kazin, in The Works of Anne Frank, *comment on Anne Frank's enduring strength:*

We tend to think of Anne now as pure innocence in captivity. But her mind and heart were never held captive by herself or anyone, and as for her innocence—it was the last thing she ever thought about. . . .

Anne Frank died of typhus in the hell of Bergen-Belsen. Yet when one weeps for her it is not out of pity. Pity is for the faceless and the weak. Events could only make Anne helpless. And though it is a miracle that her diary and her little stories and essays have survived at all, the real miracle is that in the young girl who wrote them life was so strong to begin with.

who had provided the information—Janny Brandes-Brilleslijper, a woman who had been in Bergen-Belsen with his daughters—and confirmed his worst fears.

Otto's relatives and friends did what they could to comfort the grief-stricken man. His brother Robert wrote, "The only consolation is the short years of happiness you gave to each other. They don't suffer anymore, but your lot is to carry on in life and not to despair and to cherish the remembrance of your dear ones."[67]

Receiving the Diary

On the day Otto learned of his daughters' deaths, Miep gave him a gift: Anne's writings that she and Bep had collected after the raid. She told Otto, "This is the testament of your daughter."[68]

Miep had kept these papers in her desk drawer for nine months, unread. She later recalled her reasons for keeping them:

> In the first place, I did not want it to be found by the Nazis. After Jews were arrested, the Nazis would return to take their furniture and other belongings. The second reason was that I wanted to surprise Anne if she would return. . . . Everybody felt that the Nazis would be defeated. So I had high hopes that Anne would come

When British troops liberated Bergen-Belsen in April 1945, they found thousands of starving and ill prisoners. In July Otto Frank learned his daughters were not among the camp's survivors.

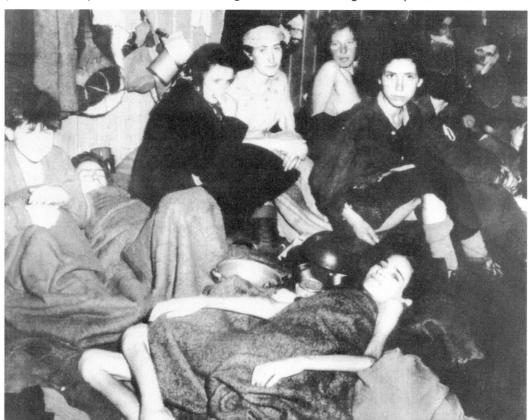

"So Indescribably Exciting"

Otto Frank was overcome with emotion when presented with Anne's diary after the war. He described this in a letter to relatives in Switzerland (the passage is reprinted in Carol Ann Lee's The Hidden Life of Otto Frank*):*

What I'm reading in her book is so indescribably exciting, and I read on and on. I cannot explain it to you! I've not finished reading it yet, and I want to read it right through before I make some excerpts or translations for you. She writes about her growing up with incredible self-criticism. Even if it hadn't been written by her, it would have interested me. What a great pity that this life had to go....

It's just so astonishing. Somebody has begun copying out the 'fairytales book' [of short stories] that she wrote because I don't want to let it out of my hands for a moment, and it is being translated into German for you. I never allow the diary out of my sight because there is so much in it that no one else should read. But I will make excerpts from this.

back. I wanted to hear her say, 'Oh Miep, my diary![69]

Miep also stated that it was lucky she had not read Anne's diary during the Nazi occupation. If she had known its contents, she would have had to destroy it since it contained material that was, at the time, dangerous for those about whom Anne had written.

The gift of the diary was a huge and unexpected surprise to Otto. Anne had occasionally read a passage from her writings out loud, but Otto had no idea of the diary's extent and depth. Now, he realized that it truly was a complete and heartbreaking picture of what it was like to hide in terror for two years.

The diary was a revelation in another way. It opened Otto's eyes to how much

his daughter had matured during her years in the annex. He recalled, "Anne developed under our eyes in that room, but we went on treating her as though she was still a giddy little girl. All of us were too wrapped up in our own troubles to give her the understanding that she needed."[70]

Editing the Diary

Although he was trying to restart his business, Otto became increasingly preoccupied with the diary. He spent much of his time putting it in order, collating the various pieces of paper and making the manuscript manageable.

From the first entries until those dating from late March 1944, Otto had two versions to work from. These two versions included the original, private diary as well as the revised, "public" versions that Anne had been hoping to turn into a book. Then, from March 1944 onward, there was only a single version. This was because it had been at that point that she had switched from writing a personal diary to creating something for others to see.

Otto set about preparing a coherent version from these confusing manuscripts. He decided to keep the pseudonyms Anne had planned to use, since some of the people mentioned were still alive. However, he made editorial changes in other ways, for instance, correcting some of Anne's spelling and grammar.

He also omitted some passages that dealt with highly personal topics, including sexually explicit passages and Anne's frequent harsh words about Edith and others. In fact, Anne herself had edited many of these when she started revising her original diary.

Otto asked a friend to type up his edited version, and he gave copies to several friends and relatives. At first, he planned to do nothing more. It would be simply a small, private memorial to Anne and the rest of his family. Miep Gies commented, "So much had been lost, but now Anne's voice would never be lost."[71]

The First Published Edition

As the world knows, the diary was fated to become much more. Its transformation from a private memorial into a public and much-loved document began with one of the friends who read it. Kurt Baschwitz, a professor of public relations

and advertising, was stunned by the manuscript, proclaiming it "the most moving document about that time I know, and a literary masterpiece as well."[72]

The professor urged Otto to publish the diary so that a wider audience could appreciate it. Otto agreed to look for a publisher. However, this proved difficult. Perhaps the war was too fresh in the public mind, and publishers were reluctant to take a chance. In time, however, a Dutch publishing house, Contact, agreed to print a modest edition of fifteen hundred copies in the spring of 1947.

Contact was a conservative press. At its request, Otto edited out Anne's candid discussions of sexuality. He also shortened the diary to make it fit Contact's specifications, since the book was to be part of a series. As a result, the original edition included only about 30 percent of Anne's original diary.

Its title was *Het Achterhuis*, literally "The House Behind," and usually translated as "The Secret Annex." This was the title that Anne had chosen in May 1944, when she had first decided to write a book about her experiences.

Reviews of the book were generally good, though some were dismissive. Typical of this dichotomy were reviews in *De Groene Amsterdammer* ("The intelligence, the honesty, the insight . . . were astonishing. . . . [Anne is] the symbol of those who shared her fate") and *De Vlam* ("By no means a war document as such . . . but purely and simply the diary of an adolescent girl.")[73]

Otto Frank had his daughter's diary published in its original Dutch in 1947. By 1950 the book was selling extremely well and was translated into several other languages.

A Hit

For the first few years, the book sold modestly, though it did well enough to require several more printings in Dutch. Then, three years after its first appearance, the diary was translated into German.

Some booksellers in Germany were worried about displaying the volume. It was so soon after the war, and emotions were raw, especially in Germany. No one knew how Germans would react to a book reminding them of a Jewish girl's life and gruesome death under the Nazi regime.

Despite these fears, the book was a popular and critical success. More than nine hundred thousand copies of the German edition quickly sold. As a result

of this popularity, the book was translated into several other languages; within the next few years, it found audiences in countries such as France, England, and the United States.

The American edition was given a different title: *The Diary of a Young Girl.* This version also featured an introduction by a celebrity. Eleanor Roosevelt had for decades been a tireless champion of human rights; she was also the widow of President Franklin D. Roosevelt, who had led the United States through the war until his death very near its end.

Mrs. Roosevelt ended her introduction by writing, "Anne's diary is an appropriate monument to her fine spirit and to the spirits of those who have worked and

Tolerance

In Anne Frank in the World, *a book assembled by the curators of Anne Frank House in Amsterdam, Rabbi Julia Neuberger reflects on the message of Anne Frank's diary for people today:*

In our own day, there are others who are viewed as outsiders—and many of us collude [agree] with that. They may be asylum seekers and refugees, [fleeing] from terror and oppression or from economic disaster or just from a lack of hope. They may be people with severe mental illness or with learning disabilities. They may be the Gypsies—the Roma—of Europe. They may be all sorts of people toward whom the bulk of society decides to show no hand of friendship, no tolerance.

The real message of Anne Frank's diary is about tolerance, and the lesson we find so difficult today is that tolerance can mean giving something up, doing more than speaking pleasant platitudes [clichés]—it is about allowing in, sharing, being true friends to those we do not know. Governments need to show leadership when popular sentiment is intolerant and to demonstrate that racist talk has no place in any of our societies, that hatred leads to terrifying violence and destruction, as Anne Frank's story demonstrates. The lesson of her story is that refugees should be made welcome and the persecuted given a helping hand.

are working still for peace. Reading it is a rich and rewarding experience."[74] Although recent evidence suggests that the introduction was ghostwritten by an editor at the American publishing house, the power of Mrs. Roosevelt's name and her praise for Anne's message of courage and optimism gave the book a tremendous boost in the United States.

Worldwide Fame

Still, the book remained a relatively modest seller for several years in America. Anne's story was not introduced to a truly mass audience until 1954, when it was adapted for the stage by a veteran husband-and-wife writing team, Frances Goodrich and Albert Hackett.

The Diary of Anne Frank, as the play was entitled, became a huge critical and popular hit. It won a Pulitzer Prize, and its European premiere also garnered great acclaim. In 1959 the play was made into a movie starring a young actress, Millie Perkins, as Anne. The film won three Oscars, including a Best Supporting Actress award for Shelley Winters who played Mrs. van Pels. It also featured an outstanding performance by veteran Austrian actor Joseph Schildkraut as Otto Frank.

For dramatic purposes, the play and its movie version altered the facts of

Anne's life somewhat. For instance, it showed the Frank and van Pels families beginning their stay in the annex at the same time. Also, the real-life figures of Miep and Bep were condensed into a single character named Miep. Nonetheless, the play and movie were powerful boosts in bringing Anne's story to a worldwide audience. Because of them, she became familiar to millions as a symbol of hope and courage in terrible times.

Anne's diary quickly became a global best-seller. In the years since, it has been translated into some fifty-five languages, and over 25 million copies have been sold. Among the many versions available is the so-called definitive edition, published in 1995 on the fiftieth anniversary of Anne's death. This version restored everything omitted from the original.

Memorials

A number of memorials to Anne have been created in the decades since her story became part of the public consciousness. For instance, dozens of schools and other institutions have been named, or renamed, in her honor. One is the private school Anne was forced to leave in Amsterdam. Another is an elementary school in Bergen, Germany, near the concentration camp where she died. A plaque also honors her at Strafbarak 67, the "punishment barracks" where Anne stayed at Westerbork; the transit camp has become a memorial for all who passed through it.

A huge forest in Israel bears her name. New hybrids of roses and tulips have been named for her. A Dutch postage stamp bears a familiar image, Anne's favorite photograph of herself, taken in May 1939. Anne's diary is also used in schools around the world as an introduction to the Holocaust.

Furthermore, Anne's diary has inspired artists working in many media. They have created ballets, musical works, and countless pieces of visual art and sculpture, including illustrations by the brilliant Jewish painter Marc Chagall for a special French edition of the diary.

Preserving the Annex

The most prominent memorial to Anne is the annex itself. In 1957 a group of Dutch citizens created the Anne Frank Foundation to save 263 Prinsengracht, which had fallen into disrepair. The foundation restored the building and opened it in 1960 as a museum.

Today, Anne Frank House is the most-visited tourist attraction in the Netherlands. All day, on every day of the year except Yom Kippur, the Jewish Day of Atonement, long lines of people file up the steep stairs and into the secret annex to learn about and ponder Anne's life there.

The many memorials, the outpouring of emotion, and the enduring popularity of Anne's diary surprised and gratified Otto Frank. He dedicated the rest of his life to preserving his daughter's memory. He commented in 1979, one year before his death, "[Anne] wrote that despite everything, she believed in the

Otto Frank visits a German school named for his daughter. Many German and Dutch schools and institutions have been renamed in her honor.

goodness of people. And that when the war was over, she wanted to work for the world and for people. This is the duty I have taken over from her."[75]

In 1953, Otto remarried. His second wife was an Austrian Jew who had had many of the same experiences that he had gone through: She had lived in Amsterdam, survived Auschwitz, and lost a son and husband to the Nazis. However, she and Otto found it difficult to remain in Amsterdam, with its sad memories.

They settled in Switzerland, where Otto died in 1980 at the age of ninety-one.

Authenticity

As Otto's will stipulated, Anne's diary and other papers were donated to the Netherlands Institute for War Documentation (*Rijksinstituut voor Oorlogsdocumentatie*, or RIOD). This organization is responsible for collecting and archiving material concerning Dutch involvement in the war.

One of the organization's responsibilities has been to investigate accusations that the diary was a hoax. These accusations have been made, and are still being made, by Holocaust deniers who argue that the Holocaust never happened, or that it has been grossly exaggerated. These extremists believe that documents like Anne's diary are forgeries created to overemphasize Nazi crimes.

To establish the diary's validity, RIOD performed a number of painstaking tests. It analyzed the paper, ink, and glue used in the diary. Other tests compared handwriting samples from the diary with samples of Anne's other writings, including dated letters. The tests indicated clearly that Anne Frank wrote the diary herself during the 1940s.

Some of the diary was lost until recently. In 1998 Otto's close friend Cornelius Suijk came forward with five pages of the diary that Otto had given him for safekeeping. Suijk stated that Otto had suppressed the pages because they discussed what Anne saw as a strained relationship between Otto and his wife. Otto had asked Suijk to keep the pages secret until both he and his second wife were dead.

The new material was tested and found to be authentic, and all editions of the diary since have included it. Journalist Arthur Max writes, "The handwritten pages, kept hidden for more than 40 years, deepened the poignant image of Anne struggling with the normal teenage growing pains while confined in a tiny attic in Amsterdam for two years with her family to evade the Nazis."[76]

A Memorial Foundation

This excerpt, from Otto Frank's speech officially opening the International Youth Center at the Anne Frank House in 1960, reflects what he hoped the memorial foundation would do. It is reprinted in Anne Frank: Reflections on Her Life and Legacy:

[This center will] create a dynamic meeting-place for young people from all over the world . . . propagate and help realize the ideals bequeathed by Anne Frank in her diary. . . . At the same time, an attempt [will] be made through international youth congresses and conferences to stimulate young people to discuss international cooperation, mutual understanding, tolerance, a confrontation of life-philosophies, world peace, modern upbringing, youth problems, modern art, the questions of race and the fight against illiteracy.

Anton Ahlers (pictured) is one of several people suspected of having betrayed the occupants of the secret annex. The informant, however, has never been identified.

An Unsolved Mystery

Another aspect of Anne's story, one that remains a mystery, concerns the person who betrayed the people in the annex. The identity of the betrayer has never been proven, and the mystery continues to tantalize researchers.

Several suspects have been suggested. One was Lena van Bladeren-Hartog, who cleaned the offices at 263 Prinsengracht regularly and was known to be unsympathetic to Jews. However, the prime suspect, ever since the raid itself, has been Willem van Maaren, the warehouse foreman who had replaced the ailing Johannes Voskuijl.

Van Maaren's own suspicions about the annex had been aroused after he found Hermann van Pels's wallet in the warehouse. He thought that people were coming into the warehouse at night and tried to catch them by setting little traps. For example, he would leave a piece of wood on the edge of a table with the end sticking out, hoping that someone would knock it over without noticing. He also spread flour on the floor to pick up footprints. Despite these traps, however, van Maaren was never able to prove his theory that there were people hidden upstairs. Years later, he testified that he had simply been trying to catch burglars with these tricks.

Investigating

In 1948 the Dutch government made the first official inquiry into the case. Records from the time showed that an unknown person received from the Nazis seven and one-half guilders per person, a total of sixty guilders—a paltry sum worth just over three hundred dollars today—for betraying the eight people in the annex. Otto Frank had the right to investigate further, but he declined. Perhaps he simply did not have the heart to pursue such a painful subject.

In 1963 another investigation into the case also proved inconclusive. As with the earlier inquiry, van Maaren was a prime suspect, but there was no hard evidence. The retired warehouseman died in 1971, having professed his innocence until the end.

Again in 2002 and 2003, the Dutch government reopened the investigation in response to claims made in a recent book. *The Hidden Life of Otto Frank*, by

Chilean president Ricardo Lagos views an Anne Frank display at a Santiago museum. Anne Frank's story and diary have touched the lives of people all over the world.

English author Carol Ann Lee, pointed a finger at Anton (Tonny) Ahlers. Lee asserts that Ahlers, a Dutch Nazi, was blackmailing Otto Frank over sales of pectin and sausage spices that the businessman allegedly made to the German army before he went into hiding. However, the Dutch government concluded that Lee's book was based purely on speculation, and that she had not investigated her sources thoroughly.

An Enduring Symbol

In the years since the world became aware of Anne Frank, she has become an enduring symbol. Her story, sadly, is not unique. However, because her eloquent diary has survived, Anne has come to represent all the anonymous victims of the war, especially the young people.

Anne's story helps people today grasp the larger picture of the war's horrors. Her writing turns a huge, impersonal nightmare into something anyone can relate to. Journalist Len Barcousky notes, "It was Anne's writing . . . that first put a human face on the Holocaust, transforming horrifying statistics into fascinating, feuding, flawed individuals."[77]

Anne Frank, like all individuals, was imperfect. She started her diary as a fickle adolescent, a typical kid with typically self-centered concerns. She grew up extraordinarily fast, however. By the time she wrote her diary's final entries, some two years after beginning it, she was an adult—and a heroine for the ages.

Notes

Introduction: The Spirit of Anne Frank

1. Anne Frank, *The Diary of a Young Girl: The Definitive Edition.* New York: Doubleday, 1995, p. 332.
2. Quoted in Robert G.L. Waite, *The Psychopathic God: Adolf Hitler.* New York: Da Capo Press, 1993, p. 75.
3. Ernst Schnabel, *Anne Frank: A Portrait in Courage.* New York: Harcourt, Brace & World, 1958, p. 17.
4. Anna Quindlen, "Introduction," in Ruud van der Rol and Rian Verhoeven, *Anne Frank: Beyond the Diary: A Photographic Remembrance.* New York: Viking, 1993, p. ix.
5. Ann Birstein and Alfred Kazin, "Introduction," in Anne Frank, *The Works of Anne Frank.* New York: Doubleday, 1959, p. 15.
6. Quoted in Hyman A. Enzer and Sandra Solotaroff-Enzer, eds, *Anne Frank: Reflections on Her Life and Legacy.* Urbana and Chicago: University of Illinois Press, 2000, p. 21.

Chapter One: Life Before Confinement

7. Quoted in Carol Ann Lee, *The Hidden Life of Otto Frank.* New York, Viking, 2000, p. 7.
8. Quoted in Martin Gilbert, *Never Again: A History of the Holocaust.* New York: Universe, 2000, p. 20.

9. Quoted in Gilbert, *Never Again: A History of the Holocaust*, p. 32.
10. Melissa Müller, *Anne Frank: The Biography.* New York: Henry Holt, 1998, p. 85.
11. Quoted in Schnabel, *Anne Frank: A Portrait in Courage*, p. 52.
12. Miep Gies, *Anne Frank Remembered.* New York: Simon and Schuster, 1987, pp. 37–39.
13. Quoted in Müller, *Anne Frank: The Biography*, p. 124.
14. Quoted in Schnabel, *Anne Frank: A Portrait in Courage*, p. 124.

Chapter Two: The Hiding Begins

15. Quoted in Lee, *The Hidden Life of Otto Frank*, p. 52.
16. Müller, *Anne Frank: The Biography*, p. 157.
17. Frank, *The Diary of a Young Girl: The Definitive Edition*, p. 1.
18. Quoted in van der Rol and Verhoeven, *Anne Frank: Beyond the Diary: A Photographic Remembrance*, p. 4.
19. Gies, *Anne Frank Remembered*, p. 95.
20. Quoted in van der Rol and Verhoeven, *Anne Frank: Beyond the Diary: A Photographic Remembrance*, p. 43.
21. Quoted in Müller, *Anne Frank: The Biography*, p. 157.

22. Gies, *Anne Frank Remembered*, p. 98.
23. Frank, *The Diary of a Young Girl: The Definitive Edition*, p. 18.

Chapter Three: Life in the Annex

24. Frank, *The Diary of a Young Girl: The Definitive Edition*, p. 26.
25. Gies, *Anne Frank Remembered*, p. 136.
26. Müller, *Anne Frank: The Biography*, p. 188.
27. Quoted in van der Rol and Verhoeven, *Anne Frank: Beyond the Diary: A Photographic Remembrance*, p. 57.
28. Anne Frank, *Anne Frank's Tales from the Secret Annex.* New York: Bantam, 1994, p. 123.
29. Quoted in John Follain, "Still Seeking Anne Frank's Betrayer," *Ottawa Citizen*, February 24, 2003. http://hmm.us-comments-8943.html. p. A12.
30. Schnabel, *Anne Frank: A Portrait in Courage*, 1958, p. 96.
31. Gies, *Anne Frank Remembered*, p. 84.
32. Frank, *The Diary of a Young Girl: The Definitive Edition*, p. 152.
33. Quoted in Müller, *Anne Frank: The Biography*, p. 219.
34. Gies, *Anne Frank Remembered*, pp. 66–150.
35. Frank, *The Diary of a Young Girl: The Definitive Edition*, p. 327.
36. Frank, *The Diary of a Young Girl: The Definitive Edition*, p. 101.

Chapter Four: Keeping the Diary

37. Birstein and Kazin, "Introduction," pp. 11–12.
38. Quoted in Joyce Apsel, "A diary Is One Way to Get Acquainted with Yourself," *St. Petersburg Times*, November 1, 1999. www.sptimes.com-news-110199-news_pf/Floridian-A_diary_is_one_way_to.html.
39. Quoted in Catherine A. Bernard, "Women Writing the Holocaust," *Modern Thought and Literature*, Winter 1995. www. remember.org/educate/afrank.html.
40. Frank, *The Diary of a Young Girl: The Definitive Edition*, p. 244.
41. Müller, *Anne Frank: The Biography*, p. 185.
42. Quoted in Henry F. Pommer, "The Legend and Art of Anne Frank," in Anna G. Steenmeijer, ed., *A Tribute to Anne Frank.* Garden City, NY: Doubleday, 1971, p. 28.
43. Gies, *Anne Frank Remembered*, p. 107.
44. Frank, *The Diary of a Young Girl: The Definitive Edition*, p. 166.
45. Quoted in Pommer, "The Legend and Art of Anne Frank," p. 28.
46. Quoted in Ashok Chopra, "Literature That Sears the Soul." *Tribune (of India) Sunday Reading*, October 18, 1998. www.tribuneindia.com/1998/98oct18/sunday/modern.html.
47. Frank, *The Diary of a Young Girl: The Definitive Edition*, pp. 208–209.
48. Quoted in Chopra, "Literature That Sears the Soul."
49. Quoted in Rachel Feldhay Brenner, "Writing Herself into History: Anne Frank's Self-Portrait as a Young Artist," in Enzer and Solotaroff-Enzer, eds, *Anne Frank: Reflections on*

Her Life and Legacy, p. 90.

50. Quoted in Kate Kellaway, "It Was the Best of Times . . . ," *Guardian Unlimited*, January 28, 2001. www.guardian.co.uk/Archive/Article/0,4273,4125829.00.html.

51. Frank, *The Diary of a Young Girl: The Definitive Edition*, pp. 138, 305.

52. Frank, *The Diary of a Young Girl: The Definitive Edition*, p. 336.

Chapter Five: Discovered and Deported

53. Quoted in Brenner, "Writing Herself into History: Anne Frank's Self-Portrait as a Young Artist." p. 87.

54. Quoted in Schnabel, *Anne Frank: A Portrait in Courage*, p. 139.

55. Gilbert, *Never Again: A History of the Holocaust*, p. 122.

56. Quoted in Schnabel, *Anne Frank: A Portrait in Courage*, p. 137.

57. Gies, *Anne Frank Remembered*, p. 197.

58. Quoted in Schnabel, *Anne Frank: A Portrait in Courage*, p. 145.

59. Gies, *Anne Frank Remembered*, p. 198.

60. Quoted in Schnabel, *Anne Frank: A Portrait in Courage*, p. 147.

61. Gilbert, *Never Again: A History of the Holocaust*, p. 88.

62. Müller, *Anne Frank: The Biography*, p. 243.

63. Quoted in Willy Lindwer, *The Last Seven Months of Anne Frank*. New York: Pantheon, 1991, p. 27.

Chapter Six: Saving the Diary

64. Quoted in Lee, *The Hidden Life of Otto Frank*, p. 125.

65. Quoted in Müller, *Anne Frank: The Biography*, pp. 271–72.

66. Gies, *Anne Frank Remembered*, p. 233.

67. Quoted in Müller, *Anne Frank: The Biography*, p. 273.

68. Quoted in G. Jan Colijn, "Review Essay: Anne Frank Remembered," p. 180.

69. Quoted in Cornelius Suijk, "An Interview with Miep Gies," in Books at Random—The Diary of a Young Girl: Readers' Group Companion." www.randomhouse.com/resources/bookgroup/annefrank_bgc.html.

70. Quoted in Birstein and Kazin, "Introduction," p. 17.

71. Gies, *Anne Frank Remembered*, p. 246.

72. Quoted in Müller, *Anne Frank: The Biography*, p. 275.

73. Quoted in Lee, *The Hidden Life of Otto Frank*, p. 180.

74. Quoted in Steenmeijer, ed., *A Tribute to Anne Frank*, p. 35.

75. Quoted in van der Rol and Rian Verhoeven, *Anne Frank: Beyond the Diary: A Photographic Remembrance*, pp. 104–105.

76. Arthur Max, "New Edition of Anne Frank Diary Includes Missing Pages," Monday, March 12, 2001, www.canoe.com/CNEWSFeatures0103/12_anne frank-ap.html.

77. Len Barcousky, "'The Hidden Life of Otto Frank' by Carol Ann Lee: Otto Frank's Secrets Remain Hidden." *Pittsburgh Post-Gazette*, May 4, 2003. www.post-gazette.com/books/reviews/20030504ottofrank0504fnp5.asp.

For Further Reading

Susan D. Bachrach, *Tell Them We Remember: The Story of the Holocaust.* Boston: Little, Brown, 1994. A clearly written book with many photos, created under the auspices of the U.S. Holocaust Memorial Museum.

Jacob Boas, *We Are Witnesses: Five Diaries of Teenagers Who Died in the Holocaust.* New York: Scholastic, 1995. Anne Frank was not the only young victim of the Holocaust who kept an illuminating diary, as this book proves.

Alison Leslie Gold, *Memories of Anne Frank: Reflections of a Childhood Friend.* New York: Scholastic, 1997. This book is based on the memories of Anne's childhood friend Hanneli Pick-Goslar.

Johanna Hurwitz, *Anne Frank: Life in Hiding.* New York: Beech Tree Books, 1988. This biography is compact and clearly written, although it brushes over some unsavory facts.

Don Nardo, *Adolf Hitler.* San Diego: Lucent Books, 2003. A solid biography of the German dictator for young adults.

Miriam Pressler, *Anne Frank: A Hidden Life.* New York: Dutton, 1992. A short biography by the woman who helped edit the "definitive" edition of the famous diary.

Abraham Resnick, *The Holocaust.* San Diego: Lucent Books, 1991. This book focuses on the systematic extermination of the Jews and other minorities by the Nazis.

Victoria Sherrow, *The Righteous Gentiles.* San Diego: Lucent Books, 1998. One in Lucent's series of seven books focusing on the Holocaust.

Gail B. Stewart, *Hitler's Reich.* San Diego: Lucent Books, 1994. A good overview of Hitler's rise to dominance, the war he started, and his empire's collapse.

Robert G.L. Waite, *The Psychopathic God: Adolf Hitler.* New York: Da Capo Press, 1993. A fascinating psychological profile of the Nazi leader.

Works Consulted

Books

Anne Frank House, eds., *Anne Frank in the World*. New York: Knopf, 2001. An excellent book of photos and brief sections of text, concentrating on the rise of the Nazi Party and on Anne Frank's life beyond the diary years.

Jacob Boas, *Boulevard des Misères: The Story of Transit Camp Westerbork*. Hamden, CT: Archon Books, 1985. A history of the transit camp by a Dutch historian, himself a Holocaust survivor who was born in Westerbork.

Deborah Dwork, *Children with a Star: Jewish Youth in Nazi Europe*. New Haven, CT: Yale University Press, 1991. A scholarly work by a social historian.

Hyman A. Enzer and Sandra Solotaroff-Enzer, eds., *Anne Frank: Reflections on Her Life and Legacy*. Urbana and Chicago: University of Illinois Press, 2000. A collection of scholarly articles on Anne Frank and her legacy.

Anne Frank, *Anne Frank's Tales from the Secret Annex*. New York: Bantam, 1994. This is a collection of the author's writings besides her famous diary, including autobiographical essays and short stories.

———, *The Diary of a Young Girl: The Definitive Edition*. New York: Doubleday, 1995. This edition of the famous book, edited by Otto Frank and Miriam Pressler, restored the original text that had been left out in its original printing.

———, *The Works of Anne Frank*. New York: Doubleday, 1959. An early collection of the author's nondiary pieces, this book contains some of the material later gathered in *Anne Frank's Tales from the Secret Annex*. It is valuable for its excellent introduction by editors Ann Birstein and Alfred Kazin.

Miep Gies, *Anne Frank Remembered*. New York: Simon and Schuster, 1987. This is a touching memoir by the woman who played a major role in hiding the Frank family.

Martin Gilbert, *Never Again: A History of the Holocaust*. New York: Universe, 2000. A profusely illustrated volume with brief, illuminating pieces of text by a distinguished historian.

Carol Ann Lee, *The Hidden Life of Otto Frank*. New York: Viking, 2000. This book, which focuses on Anne's father, alleges that the annex was betrayed by someone who was blackmailing Otto.

Willy Lindwer, *The Last Seven Months of Anne Frank.* New York: Pantheon, 1991. This fascinating collection of oral histories from people who knew Anne Frank is the companion to a television documentary of the same name.

Russell Misser, *The Resistance.* New York: Time-Life Books, 1979. A good popular history of the underground resistance movement waged against the Nazis.

Bob Moore, *Victims and Survivors: The Nazi Persecution of the Jews in the Netherlands 1940–1945.* London: Arnold, 1997. A scholarly work by a British historian.

Melissa Müller, *Anne Frank: The Biography.* New York: Henry Holt, 1998. Probably the most extensive and reliable biography so far of Anne Frank.

Robert Payne, *The Life and Death of Adolf Hitler.* New York: Praeger, 1973. A well-written and concise biography.

Ernst Schnabel, *Anne Frank: A Portrait in Courage.* New York: Harcourt, Brace & World, 1958. An early biography.

Anna G. Steenmeijer, ed., *A Tribute to Anne Frank.* Garden City, NY: Doubleday, 1971. An excellent collection of letters, prose, poems, and artworks inspired by or about Anne Frank.

Ruud van der Rol and Rian Verhoeven, *Anne Frank: Beyond the Diary: A Photographic Remembrance.* New York: Viking, 1993. A lovely book of photos and brief text, with an introduction by American journalist Anna Quindlen.

Werner Warmbrunn, *The Dutch Under German Occupation 1940–1945.* Stanford: Stanford University Press, 1963. A scholarly book by a professor of history.

Periodical

John Keegan, "Hitler's Grab for World Power," *U.S. News & World Report*, August 28, 1989.

Internet Sources

Joyce Apsel, "A Diary Is One Way to Get Acquainted With Yourself," *St. Petersburg Times*, November 1, 1999. www.sptimes.com/News/110199/news_pf/Floridian/A_diary_is_one_way_to.html.

Randy Berkman, "The Inspiration of Anne Frank." *New York Times*, September 1989. www.angelfire.com/pq/profits/annefrank.html.

Catherine A. Bernard, "Women Writing the Holocaust," *Modern Thought and Literature*, Winter 1995. www.remember.org/educate/afrank.html.

Len Barcousky, "'The Hidden Life of Otto Frank' by Carol Ann Lee: Otto Frank's Secrets Remain Hidden," *Pittsburgh Post-Gazette*, May 4, 2003, www.post-gazette.com/books/reviews/20030504ottofrank0504fnp5.asp.

Ashok Chopra, "Literature That Sears the Soul." *Tribune (of India) Sunday Reading*, October 18, 1998. www.tribuneindia. com/1998/98ct18/sunday/modern. html.

John Follain, "Still Seeking Anne Frank's Betrayer." *Ottawa Citizen*, February 24, 2003. http://hnn.us/comments/8943.html.

Kate Kellaway, "It Was the Best of Times . . . ," *Guardian Unlimited*, Sunday, January 28, 2001. www.guardian.co.uk/Archive/Article/0,4273,4125829.00.html.

Arthur Max, "New Edition of Anne Frank Diary Includes Missing Pages," March 12, 2001. www.canoe.com/CNEWSFeatures0103/12_annefrank-ap.html.

Web Sites

Anne Frank House (www.annefrank.nl/ned/default2.html) This is the official Web site of the organization that maintains the Annex at 263 Prinsengracht.

Books at Random—The Diary of a Young Girl: Readers' Group Companion (www.randomhouse.com/resources/bookgroup/annefrank_bgc.html). This site is maintained by the publishers of Anne Frank's diary, as a guide to teachers, students, and other readers.

Simon Wiesenthal Center Multimedia Learning Center Online (http://motlc.wiesenthal.com). The Wiesenthal Center is a noted center for education on the Holocaust.

INDEX

PICTURE CREDITS

Cover Photo:© Hulton/Archive by Getty
© AP/Wide World Photos, 22, 72, 80, 92, 93
© Bettmann/CORBIS, 32, 36, 55, 70, 84, 90
© Blackbirch Press, 23, 25, 28, 34, 77
© Todd A. Gipstein/CORBIS, 87
© Hulton/Archive by Getty Images, 13, 38, 40, 65, 66
© Chris Jouan, 45, 53, 61, 63, 64
© Library of Congress, 51
© Photofest, 11, 17, 42, 59
© USHMM Photo Archive, 19
© Simon Wiesenthal Center Archives, 75
© Yad Vashem Archives, 48

About the Author

Adam Woog is the author of nearly forty books for adults, young adults, and children. His titles for Lucent include books on rock and roll, Elizabethan theater, Roosevelt and the New Deal, and famous gangsters. Woog lives with his wife and daughter in his hometown of Seattle, Washington.